He is a man of solitude. His world is that of the quiet and distilled. Each night, he sits at his desk as the clock strikes midnight. He journeys inward to that bottomless pit of conflict, prompted by memory, in search of an image fused with the imagination in order to reveal truth through character and the creative narrative process. The words become sentences and they are formed. And so it all begins. This was his first attempt and successful completion of a full-length book. His name is Daniel C.A. Christianson.

Dear N,

I dedicate the words on these pages drenched in the cloak of my melancholy to you, my great love. Has there ever been a light so illuminating, a smile so effervescent? We walked together hand in hand but now it is only I with my dreams of a love I once knew and the fate of that love never to burn in my heart again.

Always,
D

Daniel C.A. Christianson

EAST TO WEST ACROSS RUSSIA: THE LONG JOURNEY HOME

Dear Brian,

Please accept this gift of my book and its words. I hope you will read it in full and dedicate the necessary time it deserves to understand my creation.

I hope you will enjoy my narrative across Russia along the Trans-Siberian Railway.

'The moments that we cherish and long for the most can only be felt with the heart and not described by the tongue.'

Yours Sincerely,
Daniel C.A. Christianson.

AUSTIN MACAULEY PUBLISHERS™

LONDON * CAMBRIDGE * NEW YORK * SHARJAH

A CIP catalogue record for this title is available from the British Library.

ISBN 9781035851652 (Paperback)
ISBN 9781035851669 (Hardback)
ISBN 9781035851683 (ePub e-book)
ISBN 9781035851676 (Audiobook)

www.austinmacauley.com

First Published 2024
Austin Macauley Publishers Ltd®
1 Canada Square
Canary Wharf
London
E14 5AA

I offer my deepest gratitude and sincere thanks to my parents, Thomas and Mary Cooney, for having created me and for providing a secure and loving environment in which to grow into a human being of substance and purpose. I would like to thank Professor Daniel Carey from The English Department at The University of Galway. I took a course in travel literature as part of my master's degree and for twelve weeks I got to research and write a paper on The Trans-Siberian Railway. The seeds of inquiry were sown and remained within me. I would like to thank my friend and poet, Mr Graham Gillespie, who listened with patience and intent as I read various scenes to him during the initial and raw state of my manuscript. Graham later assisted with the synopsis of my creation for which I am sincerely grateful. I want to thank my special friend, Riya Aneja, who has inspired me to believe in myself and the words that I create. She always asked about my manuscript and wondered when it would be published. How can one quantify the magnitude of a friendship? I have one special friend in Riya.

I am indebted to my publisher Austin Macauley Publishers. They were the first publisher I came across after the completion of my manuscript but crucially they were the first to reply and a reply with substance. I am a writer, but they have given me the opportunity to be an author. Certain individuals come along for a writer during critical moments of the writing journey and Jerry Jenkins was one such individual. I have never met him but his regular messages to my inbox with advice on writing left an indelible mark on me. I followed such advice to their natural conclusion. I have full trust in him both as a person and as a writer.

I give thanks to the great energy source behind everything in this world. It has granted me the health to rise each day and the strength of mind, character and stamina to sit at my desk each night when everything was quiet and waiting for a response to emerge. There are many things that I like in this world and some of them I am even good at but none of them make me feel truly happy and alive like writing does. Writing has always been with me like a coveted shadow lingering over my soul waiting for me to answer. Writing has been with me during the significant moments of my life. It was there during the happy and sacred moments but more imperatively it was there when I was at my lowest and in despair. It was at those moments when I put pen to paper as I was cleaving to life and began to create. Writing, for me, is the true connection of the duality between the inner self and how it understands and makes sense of the external self and the world beyond.

Disclaimer

The following memoir is based on a non-fictional journey but with fictional narratives interspersed throughout. The views expressed in this memoir are solely those of the author.

Table of Contents

Preface

Dear reader or can I be presumptuous and say readers. If you have reached this point maybe I can entice you to turn the page and begin to read my story. Let me tell you upfront that I have already broken the golden rule of the non-contractual agreement between writer and reader for a non-fictional story and the promise of a writer to tell its story as it was actually lived. The non-fictional journey of the protagonist is real as is the large geographical canvas of Russia where the hero of this tale crosses. The reader will get to experience what the narrator divulged as it was actually lived but as the writer of this memoir I chose to create various fictional narratives throughout and it was done so because I wanted to show the metamorphosis of the protagonist as he was moving along his physical sojourn but crucially the change begins for his psychological and spiritual journey. I didn't set out to write it in this manner but the inward migration of the protagonist demanded to be revealed and such revelations of the loss of his love and the pain that lingers within caused a fusion of the creative synergy between the real and the fictional. I trust that the reader will be able to identify such moments of creative fiction within the non-fictional world.

In writing this story I somewhat followed the mantra of my predecessors in 'writing to please one person.' However, I altered this and I instead focussed on the one person but that person is the pivotal element of the narrative and at the heart of the exploration for the protagonist. She is the inspiration for the birth of these words.

This was my first completion of a book and I now want to enter the arena of all those writers who inspired me through their words to create from invention. I cannot be those writers. I can only create from within my own self; my own humanity even if it is a humanity that is flawed. When I am confronted with the dark forces in this world as I stare at my own reflection in the mirror I am attacked with the words 'you're no good; you are a failure, you are not an individual' but then another voice calls out from the light and shouts 'wake up and be authentic, be an individual with purpose' and the only way I can answer such a call is to turn inward where my soul resides and begin to create words from my imagination and my memory. This is the very beginning when a writer comes out from the darkness into the light before a pen is placed into its hand.

You see reader or readers, we are not so different. You are also on your own unique journey. It is different to mine but when you pick up a book and begin to turn its pages don't you desire to be part of that story where you feel that you are not a passenger but one who is actively involved and experiencing the narrative for yourself? The words on these pages were not magically created but carefully constructed with a combination of the internal and external self. The sweat of the physical body connects deeply with the ink of the pen and the tears that fall down upon its pages. These words will either gather dust beside other books in my writing room or they will be read by you the readers and then these words and this story will no longer be mine. They will form your own individual story as the universality of life continues once more.

Yours Faithfully,
Daniel C.A. Christianson

Chapter 1
A Dream

I was nine years old when I first fell in love with a train. It was my birthday and my parents had bought me a Hornby model railway set with a steam engine locomotive train and carriages. I spent hours in my bedroom with that train set and from that moment onwards, trains and railways became a fascination and a curious wonder for me. At weekends, I would wait at Ceannt Station and watch the trains come to their final stop. I used to board the Galway-Dublin train just so that I could be a passenger on this memorable journey across Ireland and gaze out the window as the old train plodded onwards to its destination. As a teenager, I saved up all my money from mowing lawns at home so that I could purchase an interrail ticket around Europe's illustrious cities of Amsterdam, Barcelona, Berlin, Copenhagen, Lisbon, Oslo, Madrid, Milan, Munich, Paris and Stockholm. I never really had any plans for when I would reach my destination. All that mattered was the journey of riding those trains throughout Europe. It was whilst on those trains in Europe that I began to have a dream of riding on the greatest train journey of them all; the mystical and majestic Trans-Siberian train. I didn't know when I would go nor did I know with whom I would experience such a journey with. All I knew on those innocent and balmy days of my youth in European cities is that the dream of this great train journey was forged into my consciousness and from then onward, it would become an obsession for me.

At university, I took a course in travel literature as part of my master's degree. I was lucky to have as good a teacher as Professor Carey who understood my passion and allowed me the space over twelve weeks to complete my research on the Trans-Siberian Railway. The only thing that was missing after a 6000-word paper and an abundance of knowledge was the experience of travelling across this monumental land on a train.

At night in bed as a boy, I would gaze upon the wall at the map of the world and I stuck various colourful pins along the route of this train journey. This grand and historical railway also geographically lay in the land that I was most enamoured with. It was a land of passion but also of great torment, a land of creativity but equally one of tragedy. It was a land that created Alexander Pushkin and Lev Tolstoy but also one that created Ivan the Terrible and Joseph Stalin. It was a land of the ballet but also one of the gulag. It is the largest country in the world. It is a land that they called Rus and we now call Russia.

As I fell asleep on those nights as a boy, I dreamed about Russia and about one day in the distant future that I would reach that land and cross the length of its land mass by rail. It was this dream that excited my young mind so much but I promised myself that no matter what would happen in my life that I was going to fulfil this dream of mine by riding along the Trans-Siberian Railway. After all, what is more important to a young boy than the beauty of his dreams?

Chapter 2
Welcome to Russia

I arrived into Moscow's Sheremetyevo Airport at sunrise in the middle of May but I had decided many weeks previously that I would not take this train journey from west to east but instead I would take an outgoing flight from Moscow all the way to Vladivostok in the far east of Russia and it would be from there that I was to embark on my Trans-Siberian odyssey heading from east to west and culminating with my destination of Yaroslavsky Station in Moscow.

There are three distinct train journeys across Russia. The original and the journey I will embark upon is simply called the Trans-Siberian and it is the longest train journey and also the journey that covers only Russian territory from Moscow to Vladivostok and the reverse from Vladivostok to Moscow. The total length of this journey is 9289km. The other two journeys are called the Trans-Mongolian train, which dissects at Irkutsk and makes its way southward to Ulaanbaatar and finally ends in Beijing and the Trans-Manchuria train with a destination in Beijing whilst travelling through Manchuria China. I had thought about going along the Trans-Mongolian route as the idea of seeing and experiencing Mongolia and China really excited my mind but in the end I chose the Trans-Siberian train because I wanted my first experience of this epic train journey to be solely experienced within the entire landscape of its birth country and creator.

My flight bound for Vladivostok departed a little after 4 PM Moscow time. I sat in seat 32D along the aisle. Next to me was a Russian soldier named Alexei, who was on his way to active service in Vladivostok. I noticed that there were quite a few Russian soldiers on board. I thought to myself about what have these young men left behind in Moscow, in St Petersburg and in many cities and provincial towns in Russia. How long will they be away from their families and what will their lives be like upon their return home? I am taking a journey across

Russia to experience everything that comes with slow travel but these men are serving their country, mother Russia and such sacrifice I really admire. Men and women throughout its history have always answered the call of its people when Russia needed them most.

I slept for a few hours as we moved steadily across Russia through this seemingly endless land. As I fell in and out of sleep, I reflected on the young boy all those years ago who dreamed of one day riding along the Trans-Siberian Railway and now this young boy has become a man but the young boy still dwells within the soul of this man and it will be the excitement, the passion and the dreams of the young boy who will guide this man across Russia over the next month.

Soon it was early morning and I was awoken by the sound of our cabin crew bringing breakfast. I had lovely bliny with rye bread and a glass of apple juice with coffee. Alexei and I conversed whilst eating our breakfast, just like is a custom throughout the world. How lovely it is to converse with somebody, even for a few brief moments in our lives.

'What will you do in Vladivostok?' a curious Alexei asked.

'I will stay there for three days and then I will board the Trans-Siberian train for Moscow,' I replied.

'Wait,' said Alexei. 'You fly to Vladivostok and then take a train back to where you flew from?' an incredulous Alexei asked.

'Da,' I proudly answered.

'You are a crazy man,' exclaimed Alexei.

'Maybe so, but I want to see, I want to feel and I want to experience the real Russia,' I said.

We finally touched down into Vladivostok Airport at 07:30 local time in Russia's far east. I was no longer in Europe but now in Asia. As I waited at the carousel for my suitcase to arrive, I looked over and saw Alexei with his comrades as they collected their army rucksacks to begin their new life of service to their motherland. Alexei waved over at me and I waved back and I wondered if ever I will meet Alexei again in this life? How brief and distorted our moments are here in this life. I collected my small white suitcase, which will be my companion with my Jansport backpack for the next month as I traverse this great and enigmatic land.

Chapter 3
The Far East

I stepped outside of the airport and looked up at the overcast skies over Vladivostok. I travelled over 9000km to reach this port city along the Pacific Ocean. I am still here in Russia but this is Asian Russia. I boarded bus 107, which made the 42km journey to Vladivostok train station for a mere 300 roubles. I counted seven other passengers on board this marshrutka style van. The driver made many stops on route.

As we approached Vladivostok, I could see the wide highways and it struck me how hilly this city is. I gazed in wonder with eyes half shut out my window at the sea of Japan and Amur Bay. I am very far from home now but one of the great joys of travel is that the traveller is continuously witnessing stimuli and each new stimuli is stored in its brain and long-term memory. These memories will one day form the reminiscences of his nostalgia as he traces his life and the memories that he has stored over many years as a wandering traveller.

As the bus reached its destination, I exited at Vladivostok train station. It will be from here that my Trans-Siberian Railway journey will begin in a little over three days. I walked around the central streets of Vladivostok with my suitcase and backpack in hand as I was too early to check into Hotel Amur Bay where I will be staying over the next three days. An early disaster nearly struck when I stopped to ask a taxi driver for directions to my hotel and, as I began conversing with this man, I placed my backpack on top of a wall along Amur Bay. Upon receiving his directions, I walked on with my suitcase. It was only after ten minutes had passed when I asked another taxi driver for directions that I realised that I had no backpack. I panicked and ran in a couple of different directions. I then grabbed my suitcase and ran terror-stricken down the hill in the direction I had just come from.

As I frantically made my way to the end of the hill there in the distance, I could see my Jansport backpack all alone and upright on the wall. I noticed the taxi driver that I had initially asked directions from sitting in his car, oblivious to my current predicament. I quickly checked my bag which contained my wallet including 500 Euro, my credit card, my digital camera, my camcorder, my passport and my writing journals and pens.

There are some moments in a person's life that can define how memories are recorded and that moment for this traveller was one of those moments. When I ran down that hill and saw my lovely bag, I was filled with happiness but more with relief but if I had ran down that hill and did not see my bag along Amur Bay I would have been in a world of pain and my dream of riding across Russia along the Trans-Siberian Railway would have ended there under the cloudy Vladivostok skies.

That particular moment inspired me to fight for this dream of mine and to live each day as if they could end at any moment. I thought to myself that was my first mistake but it must also be my last mistake in Russia.

I turned back up that hill with my suitcase and backpack in hand and went in search of Hotel Amur Bay. The oddity about this hotel is that its back entrance is actually the top floor. I made my way down to reception, which was located on the 7th floor. I was given room 405 and finally I was able to rest on a soft bed for the first time in a couple of days.

As I lay in bed, I thought about how the next few weeks will unfold in Russia, as I will make my way slowly by train from east to west. I thought about how lucky I was to be alive and to be able to make such a journey. The greatest journeys are those that we choose to live in the moment and allow them to be immersed in our soul.

One of life's great joys is waking up in unfamiliar surroundings without a care in the world. I slept for twelve hours last night and now I feel refreshed to begin my journey. I came out for breakfast and the dining hall was located on the 4th floor close to my room. I sat down alone and enjoyed a buffet breakfast of muesli, warm bread, a plate of potatoes, fried mushrooms, cold vegetables and hot coffee. It was my first nutritious meal for two days.

I noticed that there were a lot of Chinese staying in the hotel, which makes sense as the Chinese city of Harbin is located a mere eight hours away by bus and even closer by train. A few minutes into my breakfast and as my eyes were focussed onto a map of Russia from my Lonely Planet guidebook, my ears were suddenly alerted to a loud bodily noise coming from my Chinese neighbours a few tables across from me. I looked up to gauge the reaction to this noise from the origin of the sound and then I immediately returned to my book. It was then in a unison manner that loud burping noises came from each of the Chinese tables. It was a moment of such great hilarity and also an education in cultural etiquette from the Chinese guests to me who is not used to such bodily noises whilst eating my food. The curious traveller must always be aware of his surroundings and to open all of his senses in order to capture the embodiment of an original experience.

It was time for this traveller to explore Vladivostok on foot. My first real impression of Vladivostok was how inclined its shape is. I was aware of its comparisons with San Francisco. Both cities rely heavily on their ports. Vladivostok is Russia but it is geographically closer to oriental China and Japan than it is to Moscow, its capital. It is even closer to western Canada and the USA than it is to Moscow.

I made my way down to Vladivostok Central Square to see its memorial to the loss of life during the Second World War or as it is known to all Russians as the Great Patriotic War in honour of the Russian patriots who sacrificed their lives not only for mother Russia but they sacrificed their lives against the tyranny of Nazism.

A pretty and elegant Orthodox church along Vladivostok Central Square caught my eye. It was closed temporarily due to renovations. I don't know why really but the sight of onion domed with bright and strong colours of Orthodox churches always demands my attention wherever I go. Perhaps it is their decorative nature that catches my eye and causes such emotion to build up in me. I never feel such emotion when I walk past Catholic churches. Of course, sometimes a distinguished cathedral such as La Sagrada Familia in Barcelona or St Stephen's Cathedral in Vienna will grab my attention but always an Orthodox church will bring this traveller to silence.

I walked down Svetlanskaya Ulitsa in the direction of Eagle's Nest with the hope of getting a view over Vladivostok, Golden Horn and Amur Bay although I knew that I would not have any view due to the dense fog enveloping the air over Vladivostok on that morning. I didn't take the funicular but instead I walked up the steep incline to catch a glimpse of the memorial to saints Cyril and Methodius who brought the Cyrillic alphabet to Rus.

I was the only person up at Eagle's Nest, which was not surprising, as I had no view down onto Vladivostok. I stood at Eagle's Nest and stared into the fog overlooking Vladivostok beneath. I was aware of what was there but I could not see it, which is like the story of our lives. We rise each morning and go about our business but we never truly see what is beyond the dense fog of our damaged lives. In front and behind the memorial were love locks left behind there by many lovers. Most of them had turned to rust, which is symbolic of the nature of all our lives and the loves that we once had. Even with the erosion of these love locks, the depth and magic of love endures until mankind is no more.

On my descent to Vladivostok, I strolled through quiet streets and came upon, to my surprise, a statue of Alexander Pushkin located in a small square adjacent to the Pushkin theatre. I sat on a small wall observing this grey and monochrome statue of a young Pushkin standing upright under a few feet of concrete but Pushkin has his head bowed and his hands pressed together in a sort of quiet and reflective moment for the great Russian poet. A book is placed between his hands and with his head bowed could indicate the importance of words for the father of Russian literature.

I made my way to Admiral Square which is the central and oldest part of the city. There is a lovely park and small Orthodox church located next to the square and during my few days in Vladivostok, it coincided with Vladivostok book fair and many locals had gathered to read a selection of literature in an open mic session. The book and its words are fundamental to the soul of Russia.

As I walked through its quaint garden, I made my way down to Vladivostok port and my attention was drawn to a World War Two submarine. Its green and grey colours were as striking as its sheer size and in the background at the port I observed many warships at the exhibition. I looked across at Golden Horn Bay and saw its impressive golden bridge straddling across the bay. Golden bridge can be seen from many parts of the city but it is at Golden Horn Bay that one can see up close to admire this feat of engineering.

I spent a while at Vladivostok port and watched the many ships come and go with mainly Chinese and Japanese tourists. I thought to myself if I were Chinese, Japanese or Korean and I lived so close to Russia, I would also make this short journey across the sea and land from Harbin. I wonder how many Chinese and Japanese tourists take the Trans-Siberian Railway journey across Russia from Vladivostok to Moscow?

I continued my saunter through the hilly streets of Vladivostok. Up and down the hills I walked. My calf and thigh muscles got an invigorating workout but that is OK because soon they will rest when I begin my train journey across this land. I took a stroll along Amur Bay and its idyllic beach and observed many children running free and playing. I have travelled thousands of kilometres from home but people are still people and I see things in them that I have also done when I was a boy.

I passed by the sports arena where FC Vladivostok plays their football. The stadium was empty but the freshly manicured pitch was an indication that soon there will be life here again. I came to an Indian restaurant named Jimmy Jimmy. With a name like that, I was compelled to enter and relax my weary legs for an evening meal. I ordered palak paneer, rice, naan bread and a plate of fried vegetables. The ambiance of this restaurant differs from more traditional Indian restaurants, especially in its décor with more contemporary music playing. When I entered its bathroom, it was like having been transported to a jungle with its varied wild animal sounds playing continuously overhead. We mostly look down when we are in public bathrooms but at Jimmy Jimmy the patron was compelled to look up as the sights and sounds of another world could tempt and lure us away from the mundane and everyday toilet experience. Tomorrow will be my last day in Vladivostok before I finally board the Trans-Siberian train bound for Ulan-Ude in Buryatia.

My final day along Russia's far eastern port city of Vladivostok. It has been a gentle beginning in anticipation of the journey ahead. I walked up once more to Eagle's Nest with the hope of catching a glimpse of Vladivostok, Golden Horn and Amur Bay but for the second morning in succession I was met with a dense fog. This morning I was not on my own at Eagle's Nest. Whilst I was there, a group of Chinese tourists were present and I am sure they were as disappointed as I was without a view below.

I really admire how the Chinese form groups and how they look out for each other in such groups. Each and every person in the group is important. This traces its roots to Mao's social communism and the collective which derived from Marx and Lenin's grand plan for communism. China and Russia have much in common having been former communist states but now having embraced capitalism they are both thriving independent states on a global scale.

While I was perched on Eagle's Nest overlooking Vladivostok with my Chinese companions, I thought about how language has divided us as a human species. I would love to communicate with these people but there is a language barrier between our mother tongue. They speak their language and I speak mine and they follow the traditions of their culture whilst I follow the traditions of mine but when do we meet in the middle? When do we find that elusive balance on which to unite and break down such man-made barriers that force us to carry the chains of our divisive past?

As I walked along the sea front, I stood next to a memorial dedicated to Alexander Solzhenitsyn. It is a curious statue because the great chronicler of the Soviet gulags is depicted as a man in a great hurry, as one leg carries on and the other follows. Where Alexander Pushkin was celebrated for his romantic verse, it was Alexander Solzhenitsyn who became an outspoken critic of the Soviet regime with the deaths of millions in the gulags. Solzhenitsyn became a dissident but returned here to Vladivostok in 1994 after having spent twenty years in exile. He crossed his mother Russia from east to west along the Trans-Siberian Railway. Why did he take the journey in reverse? Perhaps Solzhenitsyn was making a direct statement and by choosing the journey in reverse, he was showing that the years of oppression were over and that the individual in Russia has now got the freedom to choose one's own path.

My favourite stroll in Vladivostok is along Ulitsa Naberezhnaya. Across from the back entrance to Amur Bay is a monument to Anton Chekhov, who visited Vladivostok after his time spent on Sakhalin Island. I sat for a while on a stone bench in aptly named Chekhov Square observing a statue to Russia's great storyteller. This monument is very detailed and captures the young Chekhov standing with a book in his left hand and a pen in his right hand but his attention has momentarily been taken from his book as he watches out onto Amur Bay. On the pavement beside his feet are pages strewn from his book and on the bench is Chekhov's doctor's bag. Chekhov was a doctor who just so happened to be also a writer. Wherever he went so too did his doctor's bag, but from this monument a casual observer can see that the doctor's bag becomes redundant to Chekhov's pen and paper as the real tools for a writer. I wondered, did Chekhov walk up and down Ulitsa Neberezhnaya on his casual strolls around Vladivostok?

This is the type of street where one needs to walk slowly alone with nothing to do and no agenda in mind. It is a most romantic street with its leafy trees and one is constantly drawn to the bay down below. I watched many couples walking together along this street. They too are not in any hurry. Perhaps they come here often to spend time in one another's company. The cars go up and down this street but it is the slow pace of walking that makes this street a most ponderous one.

I came to the place known locally as the rotunda which has many pillars in lightly pastel colours perched on the wall. I observed couples there. What an impressive backdrop they have. I wonder how many couples promise their eternal love to one another at this particular spot in Vladivostok? The sea has always captivated mankind. We cannot escape its hypnotic magnetism. It stops us dead and once we come under its spell, we let go of everything that creates chaos in our lives and simply listen out to the silence as the warm breeze passes along our soft skin.

As one walks slowly through this far eastern city, one is quickly struck by the intrigue of Vladivostok's old buildings. This is most evident by taking a stroll from Vladivostok train station all the way down Aleutskaya Street and turning off onto Svetlanskaya Street. Of all the great sights in Vladivostok, surely nothing could be more important to all Russian people than this historical sight.

It was at this site at the end of the 19th century that the great Trans-Siberian Railway began here and connected Russia with the pacific. All Russian train stations share an ambiance of character but I think that Yaroslavsky Station in Moscow and Vladivostok Station share a very special architectural richness to symbolise both the beginning and the end of this great feat of engineering. Its cream-coloured mosaics and pillars signify its strength and its pride to all people who enter and exit this station. I walked down to its platform and stood beside the obelisk, which showed the end point of the longest train journey in the world. It read 9289km. I touched the obelisk in a superstitious manner, although I am not a superstitious man but in the early hours of tomorrow morning I will embark from this terminus across Russia. I will depart the end station for the beginning station in order to reach my end.

I stood outside Vladivostok Station and looked at the Lenin statue pointing across to the station and the sea beyond. This is a very historical part of Vladivostok. One part of Russia's history intently observing upon another who played a very significant role in revolting against the old aristocracy which created slaves of the Russian people. Ironically, it was the aristocracy in the form of the tsar who paved the way for the Trans-Siberian Railway to connect Russia but it was Lenin who revolted against such aristocracy to end the chains of slavery and to create a grand collective for the 20th century. I walked up past the grand Arsenyev Museum onto Svetlanskaya Street. This is the beating heart of Vladivostok. I stood outside the opulent Versailles Hotel dating from the early 20th century with its magical pastel colours arranged in classic art nouveau style. There is such a contrast between the grey skies above and the shimmering architectural colours of the buildings along Svetlanskaya Street. I walked up to Central Square with its large Soviet monuments dedicated to mother Russia and its fight against Nazism during the Great Patriotic War. Central Square feels very large and quite barren. It is mostly occupied by young skateboarders now. Communism eventually collapsed and essentially it caused Russians to distrust and turn against each other but as a Soviet nation they fought to save their mother Russia and all of their people across this immense land. They paid a very heavy price in both world wars and again in the Afghan War in the latter part of the 20th century but Russia is a very proud nation and all Russians love their own land and would die in order to preserve their culture and people.

The end of my walk culminated outside the Pushkin theatre. It is my favourite building in Vladivostok. The warm and charming exterior contrasts with its rich history for art throughout the 20th century. No matter what Russia went through during the turbulent 20th century, art always became a vehicle for expression of creativity for the people.

Why would anybody listen to such stereotypes when saying that Russia is cold and without culture? Such stereotypes voiced by ignorance and people who never placed one foot inside mother Russia. Russia is much more complex than that. It has a bloody history but also one full of culture and an artistic expression that is fuelled by the soul of all Russian people.

Chapter 4
As the Clock Ticks

One of my favourite parts of travel are those moments spent at bus and train stations and also at ports and airports. What excites me the most about these moments is the anticipation of what may lie ahead. These are quiet and reflective moments for the traveller and time often seems to slow down and the silence in one's mind is interrupted by the natural sounds of people coming and going through such stations.

I sat on a bench inside Vladivostok Station as the clock struck 23:00. Time and its constraints are a traveller's best friend but also its worst enemy as we shape all our moments by the clock. The traveller must learn the fundamental application of punctuality. My Moscow bound train will depart at exactly 00:55 but I decided to arrive two hours in advance to allow for all eventuality. The traveller becomes a voyeur at such stations. I like to watch people and imagine what their lives are like. I looked across from me and saw a young family. The children were spread across the bench with their Disney themed baby suitcases while their mother watched over them. The father got up on a number of occasions to look up at the large red-coloured monitor to be reassured when their train number will come into view. I observed a young backpacker and I wondered if he was travelling across Russia like I am?

My eyes were also drawn toward an elderly couple. I wondered how long have they been married and what has their life been like together for so many years. The husband had a delightfully long moustache and gold-coloured teeth but there was a charm and gentle ambiance about this couple as they shared some dark bread and chai before their train departs.

My journey in Russia had already begun but these are the moments before I embark on my individual quest of crossing the largest country in the world. The traveller must always ensure that he has all his documents at hand because when we travel, we are wandering nomads. We have no set home. We move from city to train station to more cities and towns and villages. Everyplace is new and to be experienced for the first time and perhaps the only time we will set eyes on such places.

My journey across Russia had been planned in detail but each part of the journey relies heavily on the next and the most important part of the journey is the fulcrum of it all and that is the timetable of all the trains that I will travel on across this nation. I reflected on my time spent in Vladivostok. It was all too brief and I wondered if I will ever return to this port city again? How often in life does a traveller get to return to a place they once knew? I am sure the second and subsequent journeys will always be different to the initial journey. Often the traveller laments on how the place had changed from the place they once knew but in reality it is we who have changed and the environment we see and feel through our senses reflect such an internal change. When we set foot in any place for the first time, everything is new, raw, untouched but crucially unspoilt too. The place had always been there and will remain there once we leave but during our brief moments we become at one with the surroundings of this new place. We walk slowly but with purpose through its streets and we look around and see how the local dwellers live their lives each day. When it is time to depart this new place, we take a little piece of it with us because we realise that we will probably never walk its pavements again but the memory of that place will remain with us as long as we have our memories. The people of Vladivostok are so geographically far away from Moscow and yet I sensed from the very short time I spent amongst them that they are every bit as patriotic as their brothers and sisters in the far west. They rub shoulders with citizens from China, Japan and South Korea every day but their heart is with mother Russia and this I feel will never change.

How does one define a nationalist and patriot? Do we love our country more than we love one another? It is ironic in that we never get to choose what nation and culture we are born into. It is all so arbitrary and yet our passion towards our birth country remains undiminished even with the passing of time.

Time is drawing ever so closer and soon I will realise my dream since I was a young boy of travelling across Russia's Trans-Siberian Railway and in the end all it took really was a decision, a definite plan, resources, the time to travel but most importantly the desire to get up from one's static position and move about into and through a new place. Why should we put off things we wish to do in our lives because who knows what our future will be and one day I too will cease to exist. Before that day creeps up and takes hold of me, I wish for this mind and body to have many different experiences such as travelling 9289km across Russia by train simply because I decided to do so.

Chapter 5
The Trans-Siberian Train

Many grand journeys have quiet beginnings. My train journey across Russia began in the stillness of a summer's night. I made my way slowly but with intention towards carriage 10 of the 99 number train. While waiting to board the train, a young Russian man who had too much to drink was not patient and began pounding on carriage 10 to get in and find his bed for the night. I thought to myself what the chances could be if I was sharing a cabin with him? It was highly improbable but then what happened. When I finally boarded carriage 10 and located bed 7 in the kupe, the first passenger I met was indeed the very vocal man who by this stage was laying down in bed directly across from me.

I heard the whistle at exactly 00:55 on Saturday morning 18 May 2019 and train 99 gently moved off in the darkness of a Vladivostok night as we made our way slowly north. As it was already late and the light was off in our four bedded kupe I quickly made up my bed with the sheets and pillowcases that were supplied for each traveller and then I went to bed for my first night as a passenger on the Trans-Siberian train. I was no longer reading an account of somebody else's story, as I was now creating my own story and subsequent memories.

There were three of us in the kupe on that first night. The impatient man had by now fallen asleep and so too had the man directly above him. They began snoring in unison with each other. It didn't bother me and nothing could bother me at that moment, as I was living one of the many dreams that occupied my everyday thoughts ever since I could remember.

I thought to myself as I stared up at the ceiling, who needs a private room in a five-star hotel when one can truly experience travel in a four bedded small kupe riding one of the world's most enchanting train journeys. Travelling by train at night in a kupe is certainly one of life's pleasures. It might not suit everybody but I love those cherished moments of physical travel as I move steadily along to my destination.

I am so excited that I cannot sleep as I want to capture every single moment of this journey. I gently slid up the curtain to see my first view onto the world outside. The gentle movement of the train as we departed Vladivostok had by now been replaced by the full power of this 99-train bound for Moscow. I peered out as I saw the constant stream of lights which was followed by in quick succession darkness and street lights once again.

I laid back into my bed and listened to my snoring friends. I tried to imagine what will be in store for me over the next month. What experiences will I have? Whom will I meet? What will Siberia be like? How will I feel when I finally catch a glimpse of Lake Baikal? I didn't have any answers to those questions at that moment because I am the author of my own story. I want to experience it all, the good, the bad, the visceral and the insignificant. I am open to every eventuality because I choose to be. I am a young man who is free and moving forward without chains to prevent my progress. I want to open up my mind and my soul to the world around me. I do not wish to stand in perpetual nothingness. The journey of life demands to be lived.

Morning arrived and light entered our cabin a little after 05:00. I continued to rest but lifted the curtain to witness my first setting in light along the Trans-Siberian Railway. My first impression was as it had been in my dreams—an immeasurable expanse of natural setting with hundreds of miles of wild forest and marshy lands that were not compatible with any form of livestock farming.

I laid back on my bed once more and felt the motion of the train and its propellers underneath. I will be a passenger and live on this train for the next three days before I will exit at Ulan-Ude in the Buryatia region. I have no set agenda during these three days. I won't have to fulfil any appointments.

As human beings, we are always on the way to something in life but as a passenger on this train, I can simply be and live in the present moment. I will eat on the train, I will sleep on the train, I will use the toilet on the train, I will observe the internal life on the train and the natural life in the external world from my window seat. Most of all, I will write on the train as my journal and pen will accompany me wherever I reside in carriage 10.

At night, when my body is tired, I will rest in bed and dream of her. It will be my home. My life will take place in the confines of carriage 10. It will be an internal world but the external world is always there waiting to be observed and waiting to be understood. I began to settle into my new surroundings. My suitcase was placed neatly under my bed and it will remain there until I depart the train at Ulan-Ude. I took out all the provisions I needed for the three days. A few pairs of ankle socks, fresh and clean underwear, a pair of slippers and my toiletry bag containing my toothbrush, toothpaste, my hairbrush and crucially an underarm perspirant and spray to help me remain clean. Everything has its own unique place in the small confines of a kupe. There is a holder attached to the wall beside my bed where I placed my toiletry bag and there is a small table placed beside our window so that all passengers in this kupe can use it for refreshments throughout the day.

I took my first trip outside of the kupe to the bathroom, which was located next to the providnitsa's room at the front of each carriage. The bathroom is one of function ability but not luxury. There was a bathroom positioned at the beginning and end of each carriage and in truth the role of the bathroom use on the Trans-Siberian train is for a quick entrance and exit. They are made of stainless steel and a foot lever is positioned on the floor next to the toilet in order to extract our daily deposits out onto the tracks. A small sink with a bar of soap is located next to the door to wash our hands, face and to brush our teeth. No showers exist on this particular 99 number train but I have heard reports of passengers in the past enjoying showers crossing Russia. I can neither confirm or deny such reports at this stage but I know for sure that my next shower will not be until I reach my hotel in Ulan-Ude.

A little after 09:00 I became acquainted with Denis, whose bed is directly over mine. He is from the city of Gomel in Southern Belarus and works in I.T. with a company based in western China. When required, he must travel to Vladivostok and Khabarovsk. Denis is now on his way to Khabarovsk for just one day and night to solve a problem and he must return to Vladivostok for two weeks before returning to Belarus for the month of August to be with his wife, who is a teacher there in Gomel.

Denis has broken English but he is very eager to communicate. Denis brought me a coffee and shared some of his mini croissants as we sat to enjoy breakfast. It might not be the Orient Express but the one piece of luxury on all Trans-Siberian trains is the ubiquitous podstakannik which is a metal tea and coffee holder. All tea and coffee comes in a glass and is protected with this piece of old world Russian charm.

As passengers sit down to slowly drink their tea and coffee while observing out the window at the world outside, there is a common sound of clinking that reverberates around a kupe as passengers stir their beverage and sugar. It is a sound that I now firmly associate with Russian trains. The passengers who occupy the top bunks in a kupe come down to sit on the bottom bed during the day and especially so while having some food.

Dennis told me that salaries in Belarus are about 200 Euro per month and that was the reason why he chose to work out of China and Russia. After having worked and lived in China for six years, he is now competent in Chinese and really likes Chinese culture.

A knock came onto our kupe. It was my first social interaction with our providnitsa. I met with her briefly early this morning as I boarded carriage 10. She came in to take our order for breakfast or dinner. My train ticket allows me to one meal for the entire journey to Ulan-Ude and I can choose that meal as either a breakfast or a dinner. I opted for dinner, as I had already enjoyed coffee and croissants with Denis.

The providnitsa is the queen of the Trans-Siberian train. There is one providnitsa allocated for each carriage. They are mostly female but like any equal opportunities employer there are some male providnitsa too. The providnitsa is responsible for everything in her carriage. She is like a stationmaster and usually has an assistant where they work day and night shifts. The providnitsa's office is a private kupe and is out of bounds for all passengers and when we seek her assistance, we kindly knock on her door. The providnitsa's private quarters brought flashbacks for me from primary school when I would have to make the long but slow walk to the principal's office for mischievous behaviour. The slow walk to that office would be time to reflect on what the best excuse I could use for such behaviour. There is a perception that the providnitsa's on the Trans-Siberian train are stern and without character but for me the providnitsa's are a vital link along the Trans-Siberian Railway. Without her, life within each carriage would bring disorder and as a result anarchy would ensue. The providnitsa brings a sense of order to the carriage. She is like a military figure and must carry out the duties that have been entrusted onto her by the Russian state.

It was time to say goodbye to Denis as we reached Khabarovsk at 14:00. Sometimes in life people come in and share our space for a short while, never to meet again and that was one such experience with Denis. The impatient man from early this morning disembarked also at Khabarovsk. I never got to talk with him as he slept for most of the journey, only briefly getting up to use the bathroom and to eat his breakfast. Three new passengers arrived at Khabarovsk.

As my new kupe neighbours entered, I decided to take a walk to the restaurant carriage. I ordered a plate of cold vegetables with rice and coffee. Most passengers use the restaurant carriage to eat some food and drink some vodka but for me it comes with a table which allows me to sit back and to write in my journal as the train departed Khabarovsk.

When one rides a long-distance train, the passenger gets to experience the frequency of stops in towns and cities of varied size. I will only make four stops along the Trans-Siberian Railway at Ulan-Ude, Irkutsk, Omsk and Yekaterinburg before completing my journey in Moscow. There will be many more stops along the route. Some will be for a few minutes and others will stop for about thirty minutes. I am able to see briefly into the lives of locals from my window seat.

One thing that I have noticed from my window at this early stage of my journey is the considerable amount of timber that has been logged and transported to various parts of Russia and primarily Siberia. I wonder how much of this logging is carried out illegally without any regulation? Russia is the largest country in the world with an extensive expanse of space and raw materials but if they continue to log in such quantities that clearly is visible by a casual observer then this region could very soon suffer natural disasters due to excessive warming of the Earth.

The train stopped at Urusha Station which is 7211km from Moscow. Its location is surrounded by miles and miles of forest interspersed with rolling mountainous terrain. Russia's size is on such a grand scale in that one can look out from their window all day long and see the rapturous Taiga like a re-run from a favourite movie, which plays on a continuous loop for the pleasure of the observant voyeur.

Along the route to Mogocha, the Trans-Siberian line runs 50km north of the Amur River which borders China. Ever since this train departed Vladivostok we have passed by many working trains all on route to their destinations with huge swathes of logs and many other raw materials that need to be transported on land from Russia's far east and on through Siberia and then onto the Urals and many with a destination to Moscow and St Petersburg.

Russia is truly a mammoth size and very little of this land is inhabited by humans. I wonder if in the near or far future that humans will settle here due to the earth's over population. So much of Canada and Russia and many places in Africa are uninhabited by humans and yet in China and India over two billion of the world's population reside in these two countries alone. The danger in locating people to places like Russia's far east and Siberia is that they could permanently destroy its natural ecosystem that has thrived here for thousands of years.

As the train moved steadily westward, I began to ponder on the great feat of engineering, it took to build this mighty railway and connect Russia with the pacific. It took just a quarter of a century between laying the first tracks in 1891 to its completion in 1916. The great irony of the Trans-Siberian Railway is that Russian convicts from Siberian prisons were used to build this railway and thousands of them were sacrificed especially as temperatures plummeted during the very harsh winters.

What is the price we place on the head of a human being? Each foot soldier worked alongside an army of heroes, all in the name of the Russian Empire. I didn't see any memorials on route to such brave men who paid the ultimate price for such progress. Here I am, a European crossing Russia on the railway that was built by convicts and enemies of the state. What greater sacrifice does a patriot need to make for its country?

Our train will soon reach the administrative frontier between Chitinskaya and Amurskaya oblasts, which is the border between Siberia and the Russian far east. We will soon say farewell to the far east and welcome in the enigmatic Siberia and its mysterious Taiga, its autonomous region of Buryatia and, of course, Siberia's jewel, the evocative Lake Baikal. We have covered 2000km from Vladivostok and there are over 7000km to go before we reach Moscow.

Before darkness set in, we arrived in Siberia and stopped off at two stations— Amazar which has a very charming red and green wood station. It was nice to get out and to stretch my legs for a few minutes and to receive my first taste of fresh Siberian air. The second stop was a few hundred kilometres south of Amazar called Mogocha. I again got off the train and I could see a cluster of wooden houses scattered throughout the environs of Mogocha Station. I walked up and down the platform for a few moments. At every stop, the providnitsa's from each carriage got off the train but they are always observing the passengers who get off from their carriage.

As I made my way back onto the train, I passed by the samovar—that mythical and quintessential device that all passengers on the Trans-Siberian train become acquainted with. Perhaps traditionalists would not refer to this large boiler as a samovar as the traditional samovar is a small antique metal device used to provide hot tea and coffee whereas the large samovar on the Trans-Siberian train provides hot water for passengers to enjoy their oatmeal for breakfast along with their noodles for lunch. The samovar boiler is mostly situated outside the providnitsa's station room. If the providnitsa is the queen of the Trans-Siberian train, then the samovar is its king and perhaps it is no coincidence that both are positioned next to each other in every carriage. As I filled my instant coffee glass and podstakkannik with hot water from the samovar, I began to reflect on why the samovar is revered on all Russian trains. After all, it has only one function and that is to supply hot water to its passengers but for a passenger who spends many days on board the Trans-Siberian train the samovar becomes that vital link to its daily comforts in the form of tea, coffee and even instant soup with hot water becoming a luxury for the hungry traveller. The samovar also provides the location as a social meeting point where passengers from all the three classes can gather to mingle briefly as they fill their glasses and plastic cannisters with hot water. The location of the samovar also forms the queue for the bathroom and many such social interactions are consolidated whilst drinking tea beside the samovar as we wait for our turn to use the bathroom.

If I was asked to talk about my favourite moments on board the Trans-Siberian train, I would say it would be those quiet and most reflective moments at night in bed before I succumb to sleep. I enjoy laying back on my bed and feeling the constant movement of the train. How often in life when we are about to sleep do we feel the excitement of perpetual movement from a train? When we are at home, in our beds, everything is quiet and still. When we stay at a hotel room, there is that added luxury of something new and rewarding but neither of those late-night experiences can compare with the feeling of excitement on the Trans-Siberian train as the continuous sound of the engine endures long after one falls into a dream state. There is that added sense of danger because at any moment all of this quiet can turn into a catastrophe but perhaps that adds to the excitement for the traveller.

During the day the Trans-Siberian train provides a rhythmical flowing from which the traveller can heighten its senses by the stimulation situated all around but at night when it is quiet the traveller calls on that inward sense of feeling in order to articulate the distilled nature of the sublime. Many thoughts can rush through one's mind during the night but the continuous thought is the one that brings the most pleasure and that is one of sheer happiness to live in these rare moments.

I awoke to glistening sunshine over the eastern Siberian plateaux. I saw rolling hills, gentle streams meandering through beneath and adjacent to a chorus of fields filled with an array of wildflowers in a mesmerising dark purple hue which shone under the startling early morning sun above Siberia. It is truly a sight to behold for the first-time visitor and it must also be for returning visitors who can enjoy the vision of our natural environment without the need for technological advancement. This is the way that our Earth should look—beauteous and unspoilt.

Before our train arrived in Chita, it passed through the highest point on the entire Trans-Siberian Railway at 1040 metres above sea level. We arrived at Chita Station at 08:48 local time for a 36-minute stop. We passed a time zone as we entered Siberia and I put my watch back by one hour so now we are six hours ahead of Moscow.

Moscow time is always the standard one on all Trans-Siberian trains. I will slowly make up that time with Moscow as I continue to travel westward over the next few weeks. Chita lies exactly 6199 km from Moscow. Chita Train Station has a large footbridge to transfer passengers in and out of the trains. As I reached the top step of the footbridge, I was drawn toward the golden domes and light blue pastels of the Cathedral of the Kazan Icon of the Mother of God. As I walked hurriedly towards the cathedral, I saw a monument to St Alexander Nevsky which was positioned right in front of the cathedral.

In Russia, the connection between the spiritual and patriotic hero is pivotal and uncompromising. I spent a few moments inside the cathedral and scanned up admiringly at its golden icons. I observed Russian people going about their daily business but one which involves their spiritual lives.

Russian Orthodox Churches are quiet and reflective places which contrasts with the sombre faces of their faithful, who consistently kiss the icons and bless oneself from right to left and bow in sacred reverence as true servants to their God. I admire Orthodox Churches in having no pews because pews distract our attention away from our primary focus. Pews gives us a sense of comfort but to stand in upright reverence is what all Orthodox Christians aspire to when they enter God's holy dwelling.

I had originally planned on spending a few days in Chita as I wanted to visit the Decembrist Museum but I chose to stopover in Ulan-Ude and Irkutsk instead. The Decembrists were exiled to Chita and forced to build the prison in which they were imprisoned in. As I returned to the 99 train, I looked out onto the low hills beyond Chita and thought about the long and often cruel history in this part of Siberia.

I returned to the restaurant at carriage 9 as we moved steadily onward to Ulan-Ude. Exactly one week ago I was at home in Galway and now I am here on a train making my way westward through Siberia. All the world is a canvas on which we need to walk out and sprinkle ourselves with the multitude of experiences that await us if only we have the courage to say yes. Our Earth is an enticing and yet vulnerable of homes.

I looked out from my train window on this sanguine Sunday afternoon in May with clear blue skies and I witnessed the natural world alive and flourishing but for how long will this last? I see more than traces of humankind interfering in this natural world here in Siberia, especially with excess logging. The Siberian pine stands tall in all her glory, inhaling and exhaling life into the atmosphere all round her.

Over the last few days, I have noticed many small and clustered cemeteries situated in small fields with wide open spaces along small mountain sides. These small cemeteries are primarily in a squared shape and enclosed with a gate circling the graves. Many small villages scatter the landscape and the local villagers, instead of travelling long distances, bury their dead in close proximity to their homes so that their loved ones can return to the earth from where they came from.

Upon arrival at Khilok Station, a marker indicated that we are 5932km from Moscow. I am a little over 3300km into my journey and have not yet reached the midpoint across Russia.

Even though I have been on this train for three days and nights without a shower, without a change of clothes and in need of a clean shave, I am happy and content with where I am at this point in my life. A long journey such as on the Trans-Siberian train allows the traveller the time and space needed to contemplate on one's own existence and place in life. Sometimes, we all feel insignificant and without purpose but we must believe that we matter too and we must believe that the sun will still rise tomorrow morning even when our recurring doubts remain hidden. In life, it is important to make such a journey at least once in order to take time out from the frenetic pace that we all too often work our lives into in order to just be at one with who we are and to follow the journey ahead by simply living in the present moment. What good is our lives and what meaning does it hold for us if we are walking around aimlessly and counting the days go by? We deserve much more from life but nobody is going to give us that reward. Nobody is going to point the way to the roadmap on how to live our lives. We reside within our own autonomous body and it is we who must choose what is the right way to live in order to find that coveted meaning and happiness.

I am looking forward to getting off the train at Ulan-Ude and the prospect of a nice hot shower at my hotel tonight is becoming ever more tantalising. We passed along the valley by the Khilok River. This canvas scene is as evocative and as natural an environment as I have ever witnessed. The rolling mountains form the backdrop. The Siberian pine are in full leaf. Gentle streams flow meandering through beneath while life stock graze on gentle and fertile land. It truly is God's own garden all around this part of Siberia.

Chapter 6
Buryatia

As magical as the train ride is across Russia, crossing eight time zones in 148 hours over seven nights, the great regret would exist for such an explorer who does not disembark the train at least once during such a journey. I am staying in room 1112 on the 11th floor of Hotel Buryatia here in Ulan-Ude. I liked Hotel Buryatia immediately. It is large and yet there is a gentle elegance about this understated hotel and its staff that exudes class and professionalism.

My room has a queen-sized bed which was a perfect tonic last night after having arrived from three nights on a train. I would not trade the small confines of a kupe for anything but collapsing onto my bed last night was so soothing for both my body and mind.

When morning arrived, I immediately wanted to turn back time to midnight and begin my untarnished night's sleep once again. The view down onto Ulan-Ude from my 11th floor room is a most striking one. It reminded me of the view I had when I stayed in Phnom Penh in Cambodia.

Everything looks so quiet and small when we look down on it from afar. People are going about their everyday lives with purpose. We always seem to have some place to go. How often do we walk around with no set purpose other than breathing in the air and living within that moment? I will soon be walking amongst the people of Buryatia and experiencing the sights, the sounds, the smells that are so natural and commonplace for these local people of Ulan-Ude.

I was a little late arriving down for breakfast, which was between 7–10 AM and when I finally arrived into the dining hall at 10:15 AM the staff were cleaning away the breakfast table and buffet foods. They never scolded me for my late arrival nor did they refuse my entry. I took foods from the various buffet plates and carried on nonchalantly with my breakfast.

As I sat alone in an empty breakfast room with the sounds of plates and cups been placed into breakfast carts for washing, I began to examine upon the simplicity and meaning of the breakfast buffet whilst slowly eating my warm potatoes and mushrooms. A breakfast buffet is full proof; it cannot fail due to the conditions that the hotel staff sets in place beforehand.

The chef and its assistants arrive early to work and they begin cooking from a variety of breakfast delicacies such as potatoes, eggs (scrambled, fried and poached), meats such as a selection of ham, turkey, sausages, hash brown potato, a selection of bread both white and rye bread along with croissants with choices of plain, almond and chocolate, freshly squeezed juices with orange, apple, pineapple, fresh fruits in apples, bananas and pears, a selection of yoghurts in apple and blueberry and of course the breakfast staple of tea and coffee.

When the hungry traveller comes down from his comfortable night's sleep into a new environment and sets his eyes upon a buffet spread, he immediately goes to collect his plate as if an internal programme has guided me to do. He begins to choose the foods that most appeal to him until his plate is full but crucially it is full with the foods the observant connoisseur has chosen. It is quite easily predicted that the hotel guest will indeed consume all of the foods on his main plate and side plate too. He may even go for a second or third helping especially if he has built up a hunger from nights spent on a train.

Why else would he choose the foods from a buffet if not to consume them fully? It is an ideal situation for hotel staff as their primary work is while the hotel guests are still sleeping and then they wait from 7–10 AM to top up the buffet cannisters and to remove the empty plates from the tables. It is a common routine and feature that is shared by hotels all over the world for breakfast. Each morning is a continuation from the previous. The routine is the same but the guests are not.

I read a temperature gauge of 27c outside Hotel Buryatia. It is the warmest day that I have experienced thus far in Russia. Vladivostok was cold and overcast but Ulan-Ude is warm with clear blue skies. Directly behind my hotel is Sovet Square which strikes me as an interesting way to spell this name as other cities and towns in the former Soviet Union spell it Soviet Square or Sovietskaya but here in Ulan-Ude they do not use the letter I and simply write it as Sovet.

It was not long before I was introduced to the number one attraction in Ulan-Ude and that is the giant Lenin head, which is the largest Lenin head in the world. Lenin sits or should I say he perches, above a large granite stone slab overlooking the wide and elegant Sovet Square with numerous Siberian pine trees standing in all directions around the square. It is the heart and fulcrum of all activity here in Ulan-Ude, although across the road at Theatre Square there too exists an energy and a congregation of people resting next to the fountain which overlooks the theatre.

The fountain draws in curious onlookers as it releases its water at regular intervals and there is an anticipation as to when the water will be released next. I enjoy Russian squares in its towns and cities because what matters the most in such squares are the people who reside there and go about their daily lives often overlooked with one another. Each of these squares have many benches for people to come and relax and on warm days like a summer's day in Ulan-Ude the people come to socialise and they take great pride in these squares because part of their identity and civil pride is attached to such places.

One observation I have made during my short time here in Ulan-Ude is how striking the Buryat women are. I am drawn to their unique Asiatic features with their long flowing and dark hair, which contrasts with their very delicate facial features and soft skin that prods a casual male observer and makes him desire these rare beauties even more. I do feel a natural attraction and affinity towards Slavic women but certainly Buryat women are as naturally elegant and as stunningly feminine as I have ever seen among the female species.

Everywhere the traveller goes, he sees them but he only sees the shell. Will he ever see beyond the mask of the external and into the soul of the female? Each one is different to the next but he only glances and never utters a word in their direction. It is not enough for him to witness their symmetry in all its forms. He also wishes to catch their eye and communicate with them but a stagnation has fallen upon him due to the sadness that encircles him and brings to the surface the mask that he wears each day on his own particular journey.

I made my way onto a footbridge overlooking the Ulan-Ude Train Station when all of a sudden I heard, 'Hey Barcelona.' It was in reference to the FC Barcelona jersey I was wearing on this hot afternoon in Siberia. I looked around and observed a young Buryat man looking at me.

'I am Chinggis,' he said.

'Like Genghis Khan?' I replied.

'Yes, the great Mongolian warrior Chinggis Khan,' my acquaintance proudly retorted.

'I hope this Chinggis is not a warrior like your namesake and will allow me down from this bridge,' I asked.

'How long have you been in Ulan-Ude?' Chinggis asked.

'I only arrived last night,' I said.

'Let me show you Buryatia but first let us go and eat as I am on my lunch break,' Chinggis stated.

Chinggis led me to a nearby café and in we went to take our seats for lunch. 'What is your work?' I asked.

'I am a policeman,' replied Chinggis.

'I admire the police. My father worked for the police in Ireland for a few years before he died,' I said.

'How long have you supported Barca?' asked Chinggis.

'I went to Barcelona to celebrate my 21st birthday many years ago and it was while on that visit to the city and to Camp Nou Stadium that I first fell in love with them and I have followed them ever since. You see, Barca is very different to all other football clubs. Their football is directly linked to the cultural identity of the Catalan people. Barca is truly more than a club and I felt a deep connection almost immediately with the Catalan people and the football club who represents them,' I proudly stated.

'Like a first love?' probed Chinggis.

'Yes, that is exactly what happened and one never really gets over their first love. The memory of that love stays with that person and follows them around wherever they go. The first love will always be an integral part of that person's life and identity,' I sadly replied.

'When I was a child, I supported Man Utd but when I first saw Barca play, I turned towards them and I could never again follow another team,' I nostalgically echoed.

'Oh no! Man Utd!' exclaimed Chinggis.

'I can just about accept Barca but Man Utd is the enemy of Liverpool,' a passionate Chinggis replied.

'Yes, we always seem to fight against our neighbour,' I sadly replied.

'My dream is to one-day visit Western Europe and to especially visit Anfield,' Chinggis said as he looked directly at me.

'Have you any family here in Ulan-Ude,' I asked.

'It is just my mother and I as I am an only child and my father died suddenly when I was a teenager,' said Chinggis.

'I lost my father too,' I said in reply.

'It is OK because all this is temporary and we will pass on one day too,' noted Chinggis.

'Have you travelled too?' I asked.

'I went to Sakhalin Island in the far east for basic training as well as spending time in Kazakhstan for formal training too,' replied Chinggis.

'Oh, Sakhalin Island. The Russian writer Anton Chekhov crossed the length of Russia from Moscow to Sakhalin Island in 1890 to carry out a study on the convicts who once lived there,' I said.

'Da, everybody on Sakhalin knows of Chekhov the doctor,' said Chinggis.

'I like Chekhov the writer,' I replied.

'I went to Mongolia last year on holidays for two weeks,' a smiling Chinggis said.

'I have never been there but I would love to experience the Gobi Desert,' I replied.

'You must first experience Mongolian women,' a mischievous Chinggis stated.

Over lunch Chinggis spoke with authority as he discussed the history of the UK and Ireland. How often we are drawn towards other lands and cultures and at the same time how we see our own culture as mundane and insular. The people in lands far away are unknown and exotic while our lands and people are familiar and all too often broken because we turn on ourselves in order to fight the enemy that we are certain exists. How we need to externalise ourselves with the world around us in order to internalise our thoughts and position in such a world.

I walked down Ulitsa Lenina or as it is known here in Ulan-Ude—Arbat Street. It is a pedestrianised street modelled on the oldest street in Moscow of the same name. Walking up and down Arbat Street reminded me of Sovietskaya Street in Brest Belarus, as both streets share a common structure and atmosphere. I sat on a bench in Arbat Street and enjoyed two kvass—that most traditional of Russian beverages made from wheat, barley and rye mixed with fruits to deliver a thirst quenching drink on a hot summer's day.

Kvass vendors are easily found on all Russian and Slavic streets with their traditional yellow vending kvass cannisters held up with a short cart and wheel with their endless supply of this dark brown fermented liquid poured from the truck cannister into a small or a large plastic cup.

Drinking kvass takes me back to those endless summer days in Brest when life beside that fair girl fitted together like grains of sand upon a seashore. I might as well be sitting along Sovietskaya Street with her next to me but as thirst quenching as kvass is, it cannot recreate the intrinsic meaning of those inestimable moments frozen in time. Everything seems familiar but also part of a different time and a different place. I am the same, the kvass drinks are the same, the street looks familiar but the one person that I long for the most is not here and so the past continues to elude me and I have no choice but to continue along my solitary path.

I continued walking down the length of Arbat Street until I crossed the road and found myself at Odigitria Cathedral which is a genial white and blue coloured Russian Orthodox Church located across from Banzarova Bus Station from where I will take bus number 130 tomorrow morning bound for Ivolginsky Datsun located 40km outside of Ulan-Ude. I sat on a long wooden bench at the back of Odigitria church to escape from the heat of the intense sun. I observed a woman who was working inside washing all the icons with her small red bucket and a white cloth. She wore navy gloves and a striking purple scarf covered her hair. At each moment before this lady washed the individual icons, she blessed herself and bowed. There were no employers looking on to see that she carried out her duties and yet she carried out such duties with sincerity and diligence. As I exited the church, I saw an elderly and small stature woman kneeling down outside the front door. She too had a scarf on her head and was in submission to her God. As I was about to pass her, she looked up at me and put out her hands once again in submission but this time requesting some roubles from me. I gave her some coins because I felt empathy in my heart for that old woman. As I walked back onto Arbat Street I wondered about that old woman and where her family are now. Is she all alone in Ulan-Ude living on a small Russian pension? I wonder what has her life been like? What was she like as a young girl and woman? Did she get married and have a family? How irrational all of our lives are. In the beginning, there is so much hope in the light of dawn but when darkness descends the light of our lives flickers out and all we have left is our own thoughts until ultimately they too will fade and die.

I rose early and went down for breakfast for my final day in Ulan-Ude. I enjoyed a nutritious meal of potatoes, rice, buckwheat, cold vegetables, a glass of compot and a cup of coffee. I made my way down Lenina Street to Banzarova Bus Station, where I boarded bus number 130 bound for Ivol for a mere 50 roubles. It was a marshrutka bus with passengers entering and exiting on a continuous basis throughout the journey.

The key to riding a marshrutka bus is to find a seat at the back of the bus so as not to disturb the other passengers. The mountains of Buryatia were our constant companion as we left the environs of Ulan-Ude. They served as an interesting backdrop to the wide-open spaces and flat land underneath. I could see hundreds of wooden houses all along the way clustered together and the pastoral setting was solidified with the sight of many cows walking on land and throughout the small towns outside of Ivol.

They reminded me of my journeys in India and especially at Varanasi, where the cow is sacred and roams free without a single predator. I exited the marshrutka at Ivol and I walked across the road to board another marshrutka for a further 30 roubles for the culmination of my journey to the Ivolginsky Buddhist Monastery.

It was a very quiet morning at the monastery. There were only a few tourists there, along with a few locals from Buryatia region. Buryatia is an autonomous region within Russia and the centre of its Siberian Buddhism is located at the Ivolginsky Monastery. I quickly learned that there is an etiquette to follow when walking around and through Buddhist monasteries. It is imperative to enter the monastery from the left and walk in a clockwise direction around the entire monastery.

It is also important when spinning the wheels to do so with one's right hand and to never show the left shoulder to Lord Buddha. I walked around the monastery and saw a few ornate Datsuns with monks coming and going. I entered one Buddhist Datsun and inside, a young Buddhist monk was sitting at a table surrounded by musical drums as he was making sacrifices to Lord Buddha. The inside of a Datsun is very ornate and resembles the inside of an Orthodox church, as they too have icons spread across their walls.

The unique atmosphere of a Buddhist monastery is found simply in the silence that dwells amongst the places and people there and the key is to listen. How often in life are we moving about and always seem to be doing something or saying something else?

Listening was the key to the life of Lord Buddha in India after he left his home and family in order to find the core meaning of his being within the silence of both the physical and spiritual world. Ivolginsky Monastery is a spiritual and communal home environment for the peaceful monks. I noticed at the north side of the monastery that there were many small wooden houses with a lot of timber stored outside and which had a fresh smell within the region of abundant timber.

I noticed a few women at the monastery talking with a couple of monks. Perhaps they are the wives of some of the Lamas as Siberian Buddhism differs from Mongolian and Tibetan Buddhism in that they allow their Lamas to marry. I didn't see any children during my brief stay at the monastery. I did notice quite a few cows and dogs inside and outside of the monastery grounds. They were all very tame which is not surprising as just like in India the cow is sacred to Buddhists and not seen as a product for its meat like western culture views livestock.

The cows I saw at the monastery were all bulls and large so perhaps these bulls help to procreate and to provide milk for the monks and their families. When I exited the monastery and while waiting for my bus, I came into contact with one of the monastery bulls. He was searching through one of the rubbish bins for food. When the bull saw that I was looking at him, he stopped and stared right back at me. This intriguing and predominantly brown coloured bull with a fusion of white colour across his face and with horns did not fear me and I did not fear him either. It was a moment of obeisance and acceptance from one species to another under the hot Siberian sun.

On my return to Ulan-Ude, I reflected on my brief stay at the Buddhist monastery. It was a day of silence to immerse oneself into the movement of the internal soul that guides us throughout our lives. Each of us are travelling on our own private journey and along that journey we inhabit a private space that is continuously changing, as we are the mechanics of our own individual story. I hope one day that I will reach Lhasa in Tibet and to experience the many Buddhist monasteries there.

I wish to experience the unknown in this world in order to gain wisdom, to grow and become a living being of truth and virtue. Even within a world of turmoil, a corrupt living being can live a life of truth. The journey back to Ulan-Ude was busy and many passengers had to stand. The aim for all marshrutka's and for their drivers is to get as many passengers as possible for the 50-rouble fare that quickly adds up when there are twenty passengers packed into a small bus.

I observed one elderly gentleman dressed in a well-worn and creased grey suit and black cap get on at one stop and a few hundred metres down the road exited at the next stop. He never said a word and left as mysteriously as he had entered. In front of me was a Russian babushka who sat with a black bucket full of blueberries that she probably had picked on her own land and now was heading for Ulan-Ude and most likely the market there in order to sell her produce. There were hundreds of delicious and organic blueberries all pressed together and picked by this gentle woman who also must continue to work in order to earn an honest living. The passengers who occupy the front seats of the marshrutka are the lucky ones, as their seats are secure and they can converse with the driver while enjoying the view and journey ahead. The silence in a marshrutka is usually interrupted by the continuous exclamation of "asta novka pazheutsta" which translates literally as next stop please. One passenger became irate as the driver forgot to stop at her requested stop and instead stopped 100 metres down the road. Nothing is ever dull along a marshrutka journey.

I arrived back into Ulan-Ude shortly after 15:00 and made my way back up through Lenina Street. I came upon the memorial to Anton Chekhov, who, unlike the memorial to Chekhov in Vladivostok, is seated. The bronzed metal statue depicts Chekhov seated in a relaxed state holding an umbrella in his right hand and resting his left arm on top of the wooden bench as he gapes outward through his short and oval spectacles onto Arbat Street. His top hat is resting partially by his left thigh and his doctor's bag.

Chekhov visited Siberia on his way to Sakhalin Island in 1890 and spent a night in Ulan-Ude, although at the end of the 19th century it was called Verkhneudinsk. Chekhov made the journey across Russia from west to east but I can imagine him resting in cities like Irkutsk and Ulan-Ude and sitting on benches just like this one on Arbat Street and observing closely the people of this part of Siberia. Chekhov was a long way from home and even though it was still his country, the culture, the people, their features and their behaviour differed from what he knew of in Moscow.

After taking my leave from the esteemed Russian writer, I stopped off at the appropriately named Travellers Coffee Shop to enjoy a nice cappuccino and a bowl of delicious mushroom soup as I sat at a table overlooking Arbat Street on this lovely summer's day in eastern Siberia. Lenina Street was once again busy with locals and visitors and the popular treat in summer is ice-cream and kvass.

Later in the evening, I sat on a bench beside the fountain next to the theatre. I observed a young girl on a small bicycle with protective back wheels and her parents were sitting on a bench adjacent to me. They were watching their daughter cycle back and forth around the fountain when suddenly they changed their location to another bench at the opposite side of the fountain, which was now outside the viewing range of their daughter. After a couple of minutes, the young girl noticed that her parents were not there where she expected them to be and at this stage the young girl proceeded to get off her bicycle and in a panicked state began to call out, 'mama, mama.' I looked across the fountain to the north side and the mother who could clearly see her daughter began to record her with her smartphone. I did not quite understand what was unfolding. This continued on for what seemed like minutes but probably was seconds as the young girl grew ever more distressed with the passage of time.

At this stage, the daughter began to walk in the opposite direction away from the fountain. The mother then ran in the direction of her daughter and finally both mother and daughter were reunited. Their embrace was so natural and loving. I looked over at the father, whose attention was drawn towards two young Buryat women sitting by a bench and enjoying their ice-cream. I was puzzled as to why the parents carried out this behaviour onto their daughter. I am obviously not privy to what happens in that particular family. Perhaps the parents are slowly trying to allow their daughter to become more self-reliant which will have to come one day but the young girl was no more than five years old so this theory makes no logical sense. Perhaps the young girl is an only child and lives a very sheltered life at home and the parents in carrying out this experiment are teaching their young girl a valuable lesson. Whatever the reason, what I witnessed by the fountain did not sit well with me as I was a witness to the stress of that young girl as she looked around the crowded and noisy square but she could not see the people she needed to see the most in order to feel protected and secure.

Chapter 7
Rossiya

It was time to say goodbye to Buryatia and Ulan-Ude along the east side of Lake Baikal and to make the short journey to the west side of the lake and to the city of Irkutsk. I arrived at Ulan-Ude Train Station at 08:00 in good time for my 09:00 departure. For this six-and-a-half-hour journey, I will be travelling with the Rossiya 001, which is the Vladivostok to Moscow train. The Rossiya 002 runs in the opposite direction from Moscow to Vladivostok. The Rossiya is the most fabled of all the Trans-Siberian trains and is most popular with Russians. It also happened to be the more expensive of journeys but as this is the shortest leg of all my train journeys across Russia, I decided to ride the Rossiya along Lake Baikal into Irkutsk.

As I was walking along the platform in search of carriage 11, I encountered one of the providnitsa's and as I showed her my ticket, she smiled and requested me to enter. I am in another four bedded kupe and again I had one of the bottom bunks at bed number 19. There was only one other passenger in the kupe and she was a Russian lady who was making communication with me as I entered the kupe.

Unlike train number 99, I did not need any bed sheets as the morning and afternoon's journey will be a most scenic one along Lake Baikal. It is the largest, oldest and deepest lake in all the world. For the first couple of hours of the journey, I slept on the very comfortable seats. Rossiya trains are a little different from the 99 train. Seats on Rossiya trains come with a backrest, which is very useful for the traveller when deciding to sleep, as one can rest the pillow in between the corner of the window and backrest. The second difference I noticed about the Rossiya is that it did not have a toilet next to the providnitsa's room. There were two toilets at the end of the carriage which are side by side. This suits all providnitsa's on the Rossiya trains as less people will be moving about and congregating next to her chamber.

However, the trusted samovar is still perched outside the providnitsa's room and passengers continue to use the samovar for its hot water. Today's providnitsa ensured that I will get a vegetarian meal, which was not the case on the 99 train when the providnitsa gave me a plate of rice by taking out the chicken that had initially been placed there on top of the rice. The providnitsa also returned my train ticket, which did not happen from Vladivostok to Ulan-Ude.

I was staring out my cabin window at the natural world outside when my cabin mate came into our kupe and said, 'Come quickly. It is Baikal.' There are many places in the world that we often imagine in our mind's eye what they are like. When I was a boy, I saw an image of the Eiffel Tower thousands of times on TV and in our textbooks at school but I still recall that cold October morning when exiting our school tour bus in Paris as we raced across to look with innocent and youthful eyes at that distinctive and unforgettable wonder. I knew that image instantly and yet it was different in a way that all experiences are when we view them from the prism of the natural as opposed to the artificial. I exited my cabin knowing what I would be glancing upon and there she was in all her exaltedness, gleaming along a broad canvas within the natural world. She is, of course, Lake Baikal but to Russians she is simply Baikal. Many of the other passengers from carriage 11 had also come out from their cabins to catch a glimpse of the timeless Baikal.

All countries have their own particular wonder that creates a sense of nationalistic pride for its people. Greece has the Acropolis, Egypt has the Pyramids, India has the Taj Mahal and Peru has Machu Picchu. When viewing Russia, I think most neutral observers would identify Red Square, the Kremlin and St Basil's Cathedral as Russia's wonder but all the above wonders are man-made. I am sure Russians would choose Lake Baikal as their wonder because it is a natural wonder. It has been part of the earth for millions of years and it is a vital energy source not only for Siberia but for all of Russia.

I observed a father from the next cabin alongside his three children. He was talking to them about Lake Baikal. I could not understand his Russian but I did grasp the true meaning of his words from the body language he showed when in close proximity to Baikal. Lake Baikal is part of the Russian psyche. It is not only an honour for all Russians to fall under a spell of Lake Baikal once in their lives but also a quest for them because in witnessing such a primal element of nature, the Russians are experiencing the transmundane.

To see one natural wonder in a day is a joy to behold but I also got to witness the Taiga forest range, that most remote, impervious and overpowering of forest ranges in Siberia. I saw documentaries on TV before where they showed the natural environment in Siberia and the Taiga was central to such a document. To see it up close from the vantage point of the Rossiya train along the Trans-Siberian Railway was such an original feeling that I will carry with me always. The Taiga drew me in and demanded my attention. The Rossiya hurtled along through mile upon mile of riveting and diverse Taiga followed the train side by side. Each scene from the moving train could be construed as never changing but to view the Taiga one must admire the diversity of its conifers—its pine, spruce, fir, birch and poplar. These are the kings and queens of the forest range that give the earth and its natural environment the oxygen on which to breathe from their expanding lungs. These trees grow and to the voyeur they can be seen as lifting the peak towards the ethereal skies. The maple, elm and oak contrast with the conifers to add radiance and strength to this life force in Siberia.

The six and a half hours passed quickly, but, of course, they would having been enthralled by Lake Baikal and the Taiga. It always infuriates me when I hear stereotypical and degrading comments about Russia that it is cold and that far too many of their citizens drink vodka. Why do we always have to see the worst in a country in order to cast aspersions about their people? I can conclude that the very people who make such stereotypical comments about Russia have never experienced Lake Baikal or the Taiga because if they were so lucky to witness such natural sights, then their stereotypes would immediately be made redundant and incompetent.

The Rossiya arrived at Irkutsk Station at 15:31. My cabin friend was not disembarking. She will continue her journey westward and later exit at Moscow or Nizhny Novgorod. Our time together was all so short and we won't remember one another in the future, but during a brief moment together we were able to view from the Rossiya such enrapturing sights that brought a sense of calm to our soul.

Chapter 8
Irkutsk

A wet afternoon greeted me in Irkutsk and such a contrast to the hot days and balmy evenings that I spent in Buryatia. I hailed down a taxi outside Irkutsk Train Station but from the moment I stepped into the driver's car I had an uneasy feeling about this man. His behaviour was erratic as he raced around the sharp corners of the station with his nostalgic Lada. This prompted me to reach for a seat belt, which did not work. When we finally reached my stop at Hotel Empire, he miraculously called for 1000 roubles from his non-existent meter. I laughed at the driver's brazen and rude behaviour but replied "niet" in my strongest tone whilst staring straight into his eyes. The stand-off only lasted a few moments when the driver, who was taken aback by my assertiveness, backed down and instead asked for 500 roubles. I still felt that 500 roubles was a little overpriced for the short journey but I relented and paid the fare to him. One behavioural trait that is common amongst all overpriced taxi fares is after the passenger has paid such an outlandish fare, the passenger will always have to retrieve his suitcase and bags by himself without any assistance from the driver. Perhaps it is the final act of humiliation perpetuated by the driver onto its victim.

I am staying in room 209 on the second floor of the Hotel Empire located adjacent to the Angara River. As a traveller, I enjoy those first few moments upon entering a new surrounding in which I can rest on a soft bed and cleave to that room for a while with the light off and curtains closed before the next stage of my journey begins. Each new surrounding is different for the traveller. Sometimes the rooms are large, while other times they feel small. Some come with bathrooms, while others require a short walk down the corridor to enter its bathroom. Some come with a large bed while others have twin or single beds but the one piece of furniture that means the most for me is a desk on which to write on. I would gladly sacrifice a comfortable bed or no bed at all for a small wooden desk and a tall chair to rest my back along. The traveller sees and experiences such places continuously and just like the great loves of one's life, a piece of his history is left behind within such walls forever. The traveller gets to know such inner spaces but then it is time to depart once more until he sees the next temporary home along his journey.

Russia and Siberia in particular have such varied landscapes and ethnic diversity of its people. Even in the 21st century, vast stretches of its expanse remain undiscovered and unexplained. Siberia is a mystifying land of wonderous enchantment and they have an abundance of natural resources. It is no surprise that cities like Ulan-Ude, Irkutsk, Novosibirsk and Omsk would build up due to their proximity to and wealth of their natural resources. Irkutsk is a very popular stopover for travellers along the Trans-Siberian Railway chiefly because of its proximity to Lake Baikal, but Irkutsk is more than that. Irkutsk is Siberia and Siberia has created what Irkutsk is today. Irkutsk is thousands of kilometres away from its capital in western Russia and thousands of kilometres from Vladivostok in the far east. Here in Siberia they have their own rules and way of life. I really like the names of its main streets that intersect one another. There is Lenin Street, Karl Marx Street and Gorky Street. Russia has not forgotten their revolutionary and communist past but it has not forgotten its artistic and literary past either. They are interwoven and connected to a common patriotic identity. It is so interesting to move around from city to city in such a short space of time as this time yesterday I was sitting beside the fountain at the theatre in Ulan-Ude watching the many people coming and going in regal sunshine and now I am here walking the streets of Irkutsk 500km westward in overcast conditions. One can really observe so much in people by moving to and spending time at its various locations.

A new day in Irkutsk arrived and the warmth and comfort of my bed gave in to the curiosity of what would lie behind its walls. I walked along the Angara River close to my hotel on a lovely and summer morning with a slight breeze that pushed across my face as I stared at a group of hungry seagulls who flew low to pick up small pieces of bread that a young boy threw out for them onto the promenade as he was watched closely by his mother. I wanted to enter the Bogoyavlensky Orthodox Cathedral with its salmon, white and green towers but there was a sign at the front door that read in English "Tourists should come in between 11 AM–4 PM." This makes logical sense, as it will be less disrupting during services. I made my way past the Saviour's Orthodox Church and then down past Kirova Street onto Lenin Street. I stopped for a few moments at a bench beside Lenin's statue under the summer sun. Throughout my travels in Russia and former Soviet nations such as Belarus and Moldova, there are a few things that remain constant and one of these is the ever present memorial to Vladimir Ilyich Lenin. It does strike me as contradictory that memorials to the Bolshevik leader remain whilst memorials to Stalin were all but forcibly removed following the fall of communism. It was Lenin's ideology, rhetoric and timing that brought an end to tsarist rule in Russia and rightfully so as tsarist rule did not speak for its serfs.

Stalin, on the other hand, was the Soviet leader who defeated the tyranny of Nazism and brought an end to the Great Patriotic War. He was once hailed as a hero for the Soviet state but later it emerged that he was brutally responsible for the murder of millions of his own people. It is over one hundred years since the end of the Russian revolt but history has taught us that so much blood was shed in ending tsarist rule for a new wave of communism and the collective.

Wasn't Lenin also responsible for so much bloodshed or is it seen as a necessary evil in order to bring about a change in Russia? Perhaps the truth lies somewhere in between, as it usually does. I then turned onto Karl Marx Street. The adjacency of Lenin and Marx streets is not coincidental in Russia. It was Karl Marx's original rhetoric on the evils of the capitalist state and a need for a true people's collective that was seized upon by Lenin to bring about a physical change from the capitalist tsars to the people's collective through a revolt.

I turned onto Revolutsii Ulitsa to make my way to the bus station. I bought a bus ticket for Listyvanka and Lake Baikal for tomorrow morning at 08:45. A one-way ticket only cost me 133 roubles. In the distance, I saw the onion domes of Kazansky Church and I walked along the main road until I arrived at this very alluring church with its salmon, pink walls and turquoise domes topped with gold baubled crosses. The Kazansky Church is a stunning sight to behold. It dominates this part of Irkutsk along Ulitsa Barrikad. I wanted to enter but there was a wedding ceremony taking place when I briefly caught sight of the bride's white dress as I opened its front door. Instead, I sat on a bench in front of a Cherry Blossom bush adorned with golden pink blossoms as I listened to the gentle hymns emanating outward from the wedding ceremony.

Whilst I was at the Kazansky Church, a busload of Japanese tourists arrived and they began to take a lot of photos of the church. They came over to the Cherry Blossom bush as if compelled to do so. The relationship between the Japanese and its sakura trees is one of ancient reverence. The Japanese instinctively understand the deep fragility and vulnerability of this luxurious and yet all too brief illuminating tree. Perhaps in viewing the sakura, the Japanese are holding up a mirror to their own souls. Close to the sakura bush and under the high cross with columns on either side rests a white granite statue of the virgin Mary as her son the chosen one sits on her knee holding a small round Earth in his left hand as he makes a peace sign with his right hand. A copper stoned angel and eagle stand guard under the holy family and underneath them a bull and lion scrutinise one another as though a state of equilibrium exists in the animal kingdom.

As I closed my eyes, I listened to the water flowing down from the monument into the pond underneath when the church bells overhead began to ring out in exultation as another bride and her groom have joined together to form a family.

I made my way back to the city centre, passing the central market along the way before arriving onto Lenin Street. I walked down 130 Street passing its many cafés, restaurants and shopping centres. My final stop was to enter the Raising of the Cross Church perched on a hill across from 130 Street. The interior of this inviting church has many gilt-edged and golden icons that dominate the walls on all sides.

I sat for a while in the grounds of the church under the birch trees in the shade of the summer sun above. There were a few water features under the trees that provided a scenic and calming location. A curious grey furred cat came over to me and he had no problem in sitting on my lap as I am sure that he is used to people visiting the church. I sat for a while on the bench, as I did not wish to disturb my new Siberian friend. I only wish that I had some food to share with him. As I was stroking along the neck of the cat, I could both hear and feel the gentle purring of satisfaction coming from this quiet creature. I thought about my cat Rizhik at home and what he may be doing at this time. Is he resting alone in our garden in between the palm and puzzle trees while all the time looking out for any predators who may be lurking with grave intent? I wonder, is he thinking of me and wondering where I am now?

When we are living our lives at any particular time and place, others are living their lives too. We all inhabit our own private world in which is sacred to us but sometimes while we do need these moments of solitude, we also desperately desire moments of love from the brief connections we make with others along our journey through life.

Chapter 9
Baikal, Baikal

The journey south to Lake Baikal by marshrutka was predominantly in a downward trajectory cutting through a large Siberian forest. I have been getting used to passing large forest coverings ever since I departed Vladivostok one week ago. Going on a journey to see something special always brings an excited feeling as the anticipation steadily increases as to what Lake Baikal will be like. I saw it briefly from the Rossiya train as we passed along its side, edging closer to Irkutsk but staying for a few hours at the village of Listvyanka along its shore will allow me to take in its natural and unassuming beauty.

I have witnessed seductive lakes before such as Lake Bled in Slovenia and Lake Ohrid in North Macedonia but this lake is the largest, the oldest and deepest lake of them all. Lake Baikal is the ultimate natural resource. Human beings cannot survive without water and this lake is so large that it can sustain the entire Earth and its inhabitants with fresh water for many decades. What other natural resource in our world can match that of Lake Baikal and yet most of the world's people have never heard of it. It remains remote and mysterious in the plains of Siberia.

Before I set out on my journey from Vladivostok, it was Lake Baikal that I wanted to see and experience the most. She lays in the geographical centre of Russia but she might as well lay in the centre of our world because she was born from the cradle of our mother Earth. She was not built as an architectural wonder by man, whereby slowly eroding over time. Within her bosom lay the deep secrets of our past and the immediate dangers for our future. She was not heralded as an ancient wonder like the Great Pyramids at Giza nor was she added to the modern wonders of the world like the Great Wall, like the Colosseum and like Machu Picchu. She is a natural and everlasting wonder and Siberia is her home. Who can resist going on a journey to see something original, whether it be a great love or a natural wonder? I am so excited that I cannot sit still because I do not wish to miss out on one second in her company. This could be the only day in the history of my life that I will see her, that I will touch her and that I will rest next to her. Mile after mile of Siberian forest is passed until our driver edged closer to the village of Listyvanka and finally there she appeared like a silhouette, a mirage of contemplative stillness that these eyes slowly began to immerse myself upon as the memory of an image and its real self, joined together in form.

I looked across at our driver but he did not have eyes for Baikal. I looked around at the other passengers but some of them had their heads down upon their phones while others were asleep. I could not understand such apathy. We were passing alongside the world's largest lake and the soul of Russia and yet nobody could see this. I did not have any set plan for when I arrived in Listyvanka. All I wanted to do was to be serenaded as I strolled along the promenade of this noble lake.

I made my way along the shore in the direction of Port Baikal, which is a 4km walk with Lake Baikal as my enduring companion, as the sun shone shimmering the surface of Baikal. It is difficult to compare Lake Baikal with the other lakes I have seen. Baikal is bigger than the other two lakes. Lake Bled is the smallest but it has a mountain range and castle overlooking the lake and a church situated on the lake itself, making it most attractive to the beholder. Lake Ohrid is larger than Lake Bled and it gives a dazzling setting at sunrise and sunset along its lake shore.

Along the 4km walk, I ascended a hill that gave an aerial view over Lake Baikal. I was surrounded by Siberian pine, birch, alder and poplar trees as I stood looking down onto this enchanting lake.

I realised that for us human beings it is the rivers such as the Amazon, the Nile and the Ganges that provide a working relationship for its people but when humans wish to relax and to enjoy the quieter moments in life it is to the lakes that we are drawn to such as Lake Bled, Ohrid and Baikal. They are the places we row our boats in, the places we seek solitude in, the places we walk hand in hand with our lovers, the places we seek inspiration in, the places that we grieve in. The oceans are mighty, the seas are unyielding. The rivers are flowing but it is the lakes that we clamour to with our existential thoughts.

I took out my phone in an attempt to capture such a divine moment in time. We are the generation of modern technologies whereby everything is instant and there is a need to record each moment. Is there really a need to physically be part of a photograph with Lake Baikal in the background? The vain and egotistical part of me demands a moment of the decorative but the inward and soulful voice recoils at such vanities. I could stand here in the presence of Baikal and take a hundred still images but the true meaning of such moments are not the records we capture but the momentary experience as it is lived and will not be experienced again.

I sat down at a wooden bench with a table surrounded by the birch trees, which protected me from the heat of the midday sun. I took out a small brown paper bag with my breakfast from this morning. As I began to eat my brown rye bread sandwich of delicious cucumber, tomatoes, lettuce with a flask of coffee, I looked out onto the shores of Lake Baikal.

Everything is in its natural place. This lake that I am fixated on has been alive for millions of years and is it possible that she could live for millions of more years? What secrets does she hold deep within her bed? What events has she witnessed along her shore and in Siberia since man first stepped onto the Earth? What damage has man inflicted on her natural waters by scurrying its depths for its marine life and eroding its shores to build homes in order to constantly be a noisy neighbour to this serene lake? Man cannot survive without water but ironically by plunging its shores we slowly hack away at its grandeur while all the time it is the resources that are most sought after by greedy man.

As I looked upward at the sensual sky with its many and diverse cloud formations, I pondered on the allure of our natural earth. An elevation exists above and the mystery is the space that separates the heavenly from humanity. I remember as a young boy growing up in Galway how I would constantly be playing outside because everything was new and an experience to live for me.

I remember laying on my back above the dewy grass adjacent to my home and I would just stare upward at the sky. It never mattered to me if it was the sky or the clouds that these eyes witnessed. It was simply fascinating to look up from below as the space separates us in between. As a child, I asked my parents what was up in the sky beyond the clouds. My parents told me that God dwells there in his home, heaven and one day we will go there too. As I lay on that grass, I would look out for signs of life in heaven but they never came. I would watch the birds flying in the air and I could not understand how I too could not fly just like the birds did. I would observe the planes coming and going to their destinations and as a boy I wondered were they taking a journey above the sky to heaven?

I miss those days as a boy because everything was a question that needed to be answered but the experiences I had along those journeys I treasure the most. It is ironic that we go to school in order to learn facts but no teacher ever talked about our need to gain wisdom. We were just supplied with words on a page to learn in a delusional manner for the next class. I stopped laying on my back looking up at the sky when I became twelve years old and took my place in secondary school as a sad and robotic boy. I was told that I was a big boy now and that it was time to grow up as soon I was to become a man.

How come as adults we never look up at the sky anymore for longer periods than simply looking upon a full moon or to observe a man using a machine to fly in the air? We admire the innocence and the wonder of children but we know that soon this wonder and innocence will fade away because it is not accepted in the divisive world run by adults. Was it really our destiny to live such lives where we walk around in darkness surrounded by our own man-made chains that hover around our heads at each stage of our lives?

Childhood has such a surreal element but it seems its true nature is not developed and brought forward so that we can experience such feelings again as we grow older. Our adult lives are filled with the excesses of our own ruminations. The child that we once were still resides within the adult and the memories that we experienced are stored and ready to be recalled by us at any moment but we mostly ignore such memories.

Adults and the adult world have no time for the carefree existence of childhood. We see those times as having long since passed and never to return again. We walk around in a haze observing and judging one another instead of sometimes looking outward and upward towards the core of our humanity within our earthly lives. We take the processes of our earthly world for granted. We know instinctively that the sun is always there and shines down upon us, but don't we see our earthly sun as more than warming our vain bodies as we stretch out on the sands along our sea shores? Do we know that the sun is still warming our Earth when our skies are filled with clouds and we cannot see its presence?

As a young boy, I was scared to look up at a full moon because I was told that the werewolves come out at night under the brightness of our moon and would find me under its light. I had a small telescope as a boy and on clear nights, I would look into its lens at the millions of bright stars overhead. During the day, the sky was a bright blue but at night its stars sparkled like glistening diamonds. If our childhoods are simply just about our carefree existence and playing in the dewy grass, then what about its true meaning that we can carry into our adult lives? If a child grows up to be an adult and has children of its own, doesn't it make sense if this adult will share the treasure and the imagination from their childhood with the innocent children who look to their parents for guidance?

The adult, through the passing of time, has erased such nostalgic memories but they find that a return to such moments not only connects them to their children but once again connects them to the earth and to the natural world that they long ago experienced.

There is a feeling deep within me that radiates outward when I am in the presence of living trees. The trees, just like their neighbour Baikal, are also a mystery of the natural world. They stand tall but they are never alone. They live through each season just like us humans do but their life is one of stillness, energy and growth.

Man has a dysfunctional relationship with trees, just like we have with most of the natural world and the animal kingdom. Man creates the unnatural from what was once the natural by our own existence and depravity of behaviour. We see their existence often in terms of monetary value but when we use our man-made devices to knock and destroy such gentle and proud inhabitants of nature, then we begin to erode the memory that such inhabitants of nature have stored for thousands of years.

I recall as a young boy how I would climb the many evergreen trees near my home. We used to create tree houses so that we could briefly escape our living world and enter a world of the imagination. This sanctuary amongst the trees became a place of happiness and of growth. We learned to respect the life and the strength of a tree and they provided many hours of joy as we climbed and jumped from branch to branch. Our instinct was always to climb to the highest point so that we would feel safe where nobody could hurt us. The tree is a living and breathing organism, just like we are as human beings. My father always surrounded himself with trees throughout his life. He taught me how to plant young trees as a boy. The goal of such activity was the joining together of man with the soil on the earth. The digging of a hole in the earth represents a symbolic beginning of life, whether it be a tree or plant. My father would explain to me that it was so important to care for the root of the tree because without the root no growth or life can flourish. There is a deep spiritual connection between a man who plants a young tree and afterwards who lives in the surroundings of such trees as they slowly grow upwards. My father on planting such young trees would take time to pour water to their slight roots just like how we care for a growing baby in their first few years of life. When man connects with the natural world and cares for it like he cares for his own body, then a special relationship begins between man and nature. Upon planting such baby trees, my father would give me the responsibility to care for them especially during the summer months when they needed water to survive and grow. As I began to physically grow so did the many young trees in our garden. When the cycle of life takes its natural course, then all life will grow but when man becomes a barrier to such a cycle of life then the natural world slowly erodes until it fades and dies unnaturally.

I once heard a story about a town in Mexico. The mayor of that town had an idea for expansion and growth in prosperity for his town and their inhabitants. His plan was to physically remove the natural landscape surrounding the town in order to build new homes. The removal was quick and decisive in human terms. When it was complete, there was not one trace of the once natural environment that resided there long before the town and its people arrived. The story did not end there. The following winter, a landslide struck that town and left devastation in its wake. It caused floods and a storm that knocked the many homes as quick and as decisive just like how the natural environment was previously removed in that town. The mayor could only look on in his own folly and regret. The natural environment is not just a place for us to enjoy its splendour. They also provide a role within nature as they protect whole villages, towns and cities as a collective with their strength.

There is a reason why we radiate towards large trees during heavy rain and storms. We instinctively know that the trees provide shelter and, as a result, we often rest there under their tall branches before we return to safety. I like to sit in silence under large oak trees. They provide a place of solitude on which to reflect and a place of inspiration when we read because the words on that page take us out beside the natural environment.

As our cities continue to grow upward and outward, our suburbs become sprawled and it is often the natural environment that is chosen for culling because it does not have a voice of its own. The growth of human beings has reached 8 billion and our small and susceptible blue planet is under severe strain with the unnatural energies of humankind. This is very evident here at Listyvanka. This small town only exists because of a plethora of natural resources generated out from Lake Baikal.

When travellers as I are lured to such immaculate places, we become the physical threat to the natural environment as it hangs on in silence hidden in the shadows of Listyvanka. Mankind can co-exist with nature but because of our large numbers and our erratic behaviour, we do cause irreparable damage to nature simply by our existence.

The only solution is for mankind to accept the natural world as a living and breathing source of life and energy in this world, just like we are as human beings. I am pessimistic that such a co-existence can ever occur because we never have truly co-existed with ourselves as human beings.

I made my way back down to the promenade to be close to Lake Baikal. She remains my perpetual ally and she is always visible wherever one resides here at Listyvanka. The problem with naturally beautiful locations like Lake Baikal is that they become victims of their own beauty. I could witness this in only a few hours walking up and down its promenade at Listyvanka. The people who reside here are carving up much of the lake shore in order to set up businesses to cater to visitors like me. Some of the buildings look gawdy and artificial, especially when standing in the presence of Lake Baikal.

After a lot of walking along the promenade, my legs felt heavy and I stopped and sat upon a small concrete wall overlooking the lake. I observed a family adjacent to me. They had a dog with them and he was being led on a white coloured leash. The grey and white coloured husky was so excited as he was jumping up and down, trying to evade the prison of his leash. All he wanted to do was race into the waters of Baikal and immerse itself in the clear waters.

Why do humans use a leash to walk their dogs? It never makes any logical sense to me as to why this happens. Don't we realise that dogs and most animals view their world through the prism of their nose and its scent? The dog was utterly engrossed by the sounds and scents along Baikal shore but his master continued to talk amongst each other by the wall next to their car. They brought their dog to a mere 50 metres of Lake Baikal and they don't allow him to run free into the water.

How peculiar we truly are as a species. The instinctive nature of this Siberian husky both prompted and inspired me to lift up my weary legs from the concrete wall and walk slowly towards the lake's shore. I was now standing at its edge as the water drew closer to my feet. I looked out far across the horizon. Everything was still and so was I. This was the place that I dreamed to be in for many years of my life and now finally I was here to witness the transcendent amid the disruption of this world. It was a meeting of the ancient with the youth, of the natural with the human, of the strong with the weak. I closed my eyes and opened my heart so that my soul could begin to immerse itself with this natural wonder from our world. I felt the cool breeze fall across my placid face as it gently brushed against my hair. The sense of sight was not in use now. I opened my ears to listen because when we fall silent in this world and begin to listen the magnitude of our world and its deeps secrets are slowly revealed to us through wisdom but only if we fully open our minds and soul to such teaching. I felt a deep connection to nature as I stood there, transfixed in thought and emotion and I began to submit my own humanity in order to co-exist with nature. I bent down and began to take off my shoes and socks and rolled up my jeans to expose my legs. I walked closer as my feet felt the soft sands with the hard stones and bristling shells as the last steps awaited me. I dipped my toes into the water of Baikal and a cold sensation hit my warm body with a shudder. Everything was calm and I walked in a little further. The water was so clear that I caught sight of my pale feet resting alongside the seashells and a multitude of stones, too many to count. I bent down once more to allow my hands to feel the energy from this mighty lake. I began to wash my arms, my legs and finally my face in a symbolic act of the cleansing of the corrupt with the beauty and ataraxy of nature. I looked out once more across this tender lake. I wanted to capture this moment in my mind's eye and deep within my soul because it is not what we see and hear and touch in this world that truly matters. It is what we experience during these very short moments from our lives that will be cemented as memories in our brains and as a moment of the ideal combined with wisdom so that the human being becomes more than he was. On the way out of the water, I looked over and laid eyes upon the husky. He no longer tried to fight his way into the water. He had resigned to his fate imposed on him by his delusional owners.

When I am amongst nature, I long to experience this natural world in the silence of my own thoughts without the presence of others. However, a loneliness exists within me and a sadness pervades my heart because although I am happy to be alone, the sight of such enticing elegance fills up a longing in me for her. She is never really too far away. At the beginning of this journey across Russia, it was Siberia and specifically here at Lake Baikal that I was most looking forward to experiencing. At the same time, this was also the place that I envisaged a melancholy within me for what I have lost from my life. There are many precious places in this world and if we are lucky enough and our body holds strong, then we can get to experience a few of these places during our lifetime. When we get to visit a beautiful sight alone, we are lucky but when we get to visit that same beautiful sight with somebody we love, then we are special. The beautiful sight on which we experience will always remain the same but something changes when we share that experience with another. In truth, the beautiful sight becomes the backdrop for the love story between the lovers. It really doesn't matter where the lovers are as long as they are together. The lovers will always recall a specific place and will often long to return to that place, but in truth they actually long to return to one another to recapture such tender moments of love from their past.

I never really got to share Lake Baikal with her. We talked about it once many years ago and we said then that one day we will walk along its shores together but that wish did not come to pass. I am here all alone and yet she always feels close enough just to reach out and touch her warm and soft face and her comforting hands.

I wonder how many lovers come here to share their love? How often has Lake Baikal formed the background for their private moments, frozen in time? The lovers do not need a physical reminder of their time spent here, as such memories reside along the walls of their hearts. The physical image is often brought out because when we see it again, we immediately travel back in time to that very spot and we can recall everything about that moment as freshly and as accurately as we know about our present moments.

There are many enchanting places in this world that I was lucky enough to have shared them with her. I remember experiencing those moments with her at the Eiffel Tower. I had been there as a fifteen-year-old boy but it was only when I was there with her that the Eiffel Tower took on a whole new exterior grandiosity because it formed the story of our love. Afterward, I could only see the Eiffel Tower and think about her. Isn't it strange or maybe magical how the physical environment that we walk upon changes by the special few people whom we trace those steps with together?

I have returned to Paris and walked passed the Eiffel Tower on many occasions since those tender days but now when I pass the Eiffel Tower it doesn't shine bright like it once did. It still stands erect and will always be captivating but tears fall from my eyes when I pass such graceful and nostalgic places now. Those places I experience in the present moment but I think about and long for their past moments when the sun shone brightest and the air was filled with joy and a hope for what would come in our future together.

Can we ever truly see a magnificent sight like we did before we shared them with a special person? I remember sharing Venice with her. It was a long time ago but those memories are still vivid and alive within me. We would travel up and down the Grand Canal by vaporetto with gelato in our hands and smiles along our faces because we were together and all that mattered was those special moments that we shared and experienced as lovers. We would sit out and have our morning coffee and croissant on San Marco Piazza whilst fixating up at San Marco Basilica. Our past didn't matter and the future would eventually come but we wanted to truly live in those incomparable few moments. I returned to Venice to celebrate my birthday last November. Venice was different when I returned just like Paris was. It was still charming but I had changed and the lens on which witnessed Venice had become blurred. A sadness had entered and it followed me along my path. My visit to Venice also coincided with major floods that struck there and devastated its residents and buildings. The flood water that invaded San Marco Piazza paralleled with the chasm of desolation that invaded my soul. It was not the Venice I once knew and it could never be the Venice of yesteryear.

How many lovers return to such beloved places after the death of their love? They walk around in grief, pleading with the present to reverse into the past when they were together and alive in their love. However, the past can never be resurrected and the present must be lived even if that life is one of perpetual sadness. The lover as he once was and longs to be again will walk alone in such love filled places. He will look at other lovers and admire the magnetism of their love. He will go into parks and sit on benches so that he can see other lovers together and he will recall the hypnotic lure of the love he once shared. He will continue to walk as a ghost around such places of seductiveness. He longs for just another love filled moment to ease the morose but it is never granted. He remains alone in his own grief, without any love.

I often imagine what it would feel like to see her one more time? What would we say to one another? Has the anger and arguments subsided? Has our hearts softened with the passing of time? Would we still recognise one another? We are older now and the passage of time externally coupled with the internal sufferings can clearly be seen along my beaten skin. I don't smile like I once did, although coming here to Listyvanka and seeing such natural refinement fills my soul with a hope that somehow I must carry on and live a life that is worthy of the person that who dwells within me. If I was offered one wish right now here in my life, I would not ask for riches because such a life would not make me happy. I would still be sad and long for her. No amount of riches could quench the depths of my despair. I wouldn't ask or have any desire for world peace either, as such a demand cannot be granted instantly. It has to be fought for but not a physical fight with violence and war. Peace on a global scale can only occur when the nations of this world unite as one people rather than divided as nation states. I wouldn't ask for or have any longing towards a physical possession because in truth there is an inane and empty feeling with physical possessions, as every possession that we have ever accumulated will fade and die just like their owner. I could be surrounded by a large house and a million possessions with incalculable wealth but such a life would destroy any goodness that exists within me. Possessions and wealth only make us feel miserable and constantly vigilant due to the mistrust of others because of what we have and for what they want. In the end, I could only ask for one thing but it would only last momentarily. It would not be anything that I could take away with me in any physical way. My wish would be to see her, my fair one, one more time. I know it will never be granted but that is my wish. If she appeared beside me now, I would take her hand and find a secluded place close to Port Baikal and we would rest in the shade overlooking the clear and sparkling waters of Lake Baikal. I don't know what I would say to her. Perhaps it is at such moments that we should not utter any words but simply be and live in the magic and spell of such an illusory moment.

There is a statue of a couple of lovers that rests on my writing desk at home. I placed it there to remind me of the temperate nature of life but also the sweet love between human beings. What I love the most about this handmade sculpted statue is that the lovers remain faceless. Nobody can see into their eyes because their eyes do not exist. Nobody can see the expression along their countenance because that does not exist either. We cannot see their mouths, their nose or their ears because such senses are not perceptible to the voyeur. They only exist in the space that the lovers share together. The male lover has brown coloured pants and shoes. He has a beige coloured top which blends with the woman's long beige gown. She has long brown hair and his hair is also brown and short. He stands slightly behind his lover and to her left. He tilts his head downward and rests against her head. He embraces his lover by wrapping his two hands around her body and rests them at the junction of her navel. Her right arm and hand rests over his embraced hands while her left arm is positioned in a straight line and bent at an angle at the elbow where her hand then touches her lover's face over the skin where his left ear would be. I often spent long and reflective moments staring at this statue because it endures across time and space. Their love and the root that binds them together is forever captured in their loving embrace. The delight of this statue is that this couple can be any lover because of its faceless nature. Any couple looking upon them can replicate such a moment in their lives and try to remain in such a loving embrace for as long as they can.

I know logically that a loving couple cannot last forever due to the transient nature of all of our lives. We are born, we grow, we live, we love and then we fade away into nothingness. We are all aware of this fact but it remains inconceivable to believe because our ego will never allow us to accept that this once strong and living body can self-destruct and die whereby all that remains of our once existence is the bones of our lifeless body.

When I imagine and look at the faceless couple now, I replicate her and I together in such a warm embrace. I cannot be with her anymore in a physical way but she can still continue to exist within me as long as this body continues to live.

I wonder where she is right now? It is unimaginable that she would realise that I am thinking about her now as I conjure up her graceful structure along the distilled waters of Baikal. I don't know anything about her life now. I don't know where she resides. I don't know what she does in her life. I don't know if she has found love again. All I know for certain is that she is not here with me now. The truth is, she will never again be by my side in this life and that harsh but valid truth crushes my corroded heart. She was an all too brief eclipse crossing a darkened night into the bright surroundings of my soul. I never thought that we would break. How could I possibly think such a destruction when I was part of a wonderous light that enchanted my life and made me wake up from the coma of my previous life before she arrived.

When a love dies, so too does the life of that couple as they move away from the light and into another state that does not immediately become apparent to them. They will move on, live again and maybe love again but what will that future love encompass? How can I possibly love again after her? When a love breaks and dies, there is a scarring along the lines of one's heart. Such scars cannot be detected in any medical examination but they are real and felt only by the person who once loved and desires his love again.

I wonder has she ever been here to Baikal or will she come here in the future? I wonder will she walk along the same promenade that I walked along as her footprints are joined together with my footprints in a connection from the past that was familiar, that was charming, that was sacred but ultimately that was to walk in different directions for evermore? I wonder, will she ascend to the hilltop lookout point and peer down admiringly onto Lake Baikal? I wonder when her eyes catch a glimpse of noble Lake Baikal will she think of me or am I just a forgotten memory from her past whose guarded doors have been securely shut?

If I close my eyes long enough, perhaps within the depths of the secretive Lake Baikal, she will come out from and rest here with me one more time. I dream of the impossible but don't we in a world full of plunder and destruction? It is the impossible dreams that we desire most to come true because the alternative is one full of uncertainty and a mundane and relentless existence without that love. If she was here with me now, I would hold her and embrace her in these once strong arms but now fading as the elastic skin wages its war upon the ageing process. I am no longer the young man she once knew. I am physically older now and perhaps unrecognisable to that young, slim and happy boy she remembered from her past. I cannot halt the force and strength of time. It must continue along its decisive path until one day everything and everyone will have passed and all that will be left are the empty spaces and places like Lake Baikal that go on and on and on forever. As I walked up and down the promenade, I imagined that she was with me holding my hand as the cool air blew across our soul filled faces. I would embrace her just like the man embraces his lover in the faceless statue. By holding her close to me, I could try and recapture the innocence of our days together from the past. If I touched her skin and kissed her lips, would I dissolve into fragments of molecules as determined by fate that dealt its crushing blow onto our love until the end of time? The answer would be simple and it would be to hold out my hand to embrace with her hand. I imagine that we have this lake all to ourselves. I would take her out with me on a small boat as we would watch the sun set over the horizon. I would row our boat out to a secluded place until everything was quiet, everything was still. The moon would pierce our soul with its droplets of diamond dust sprinkled across the lake, covering us with its shadow to protect our love. We would take off the physical garments that cover our bodies and then take a step forward, as our toes would meet with the cold waters of Baikal. The intermittent cold would be embraced by the warmth of our bodies and the love within our hearts. As we

69

moved outward into the depths of the lake, we would now be alone with only the mysteries of this lake underneath to be shared with us. I would only have eyes for her and she for me. We would be together in the waters of our own shared love. I would smile at her and she would smile back at me as she once did all those years ago. I cannot forget that quintessential and exuberant smile that pierced my heart and left me forever enchanted and enamoured by the sacredness of love. I opened my eyes and she had faded away into the outer reaches of this timeless lake under the empyrean Siberian sky. She is not my love anymore. She is somebody else's love now. It makes me sad that we will never again share such moments together in this life. My life is that much more darkened by having the light of my life fade away from my heart.

Chapter 10
A Siberian Call

The summer sun continued to beat its light onto the clear waters of Baikal as I departed the port and made my way on foot along the path back in the direction of Listyvanka village. My time spent alongside this great and undisturbed lake was drawing to a close and soon I would make my journey back to Irkutsk.

The days spent amidst the natural environment illuminate its radiant light into our soul, whereas the days spent back in the ruination within society hinder the innate sparkle within us and instead of the light, we only see darkness. I found a large rock close to the shore overlooking Baikal and there I gathered to just sit, reflect and immerse myself into this natural wonder. Everything was in its place. The sun was shining, the waters were clear and self-controlled. The birds were hovering overhead.

I should be happy dwelling beside mother nature but inside a void exists. I looked out beyond Baikal and if ever a moment arrived, to call out and ask from the space beyond it had arrived. Are you out there, I gently called out with my head tilted and bowed, observing the calming flow of water to the edge of the shore? Where are you, I asked a second time as the tone and frequency of my voice intensified? I feel your presence most closely whenever I spend time within nature and yet each time I depart a natural wonder of our world such as Lake Baikal, I must return to the world and the everyday irrationalities of our lives. Is there really a great meaning and a grand truth to all our lives or is everything just a lived experience by moment and chance? I should sit here in reverence to mother nature and in awe of everything I see and feel but the corruption and brokenness within me also wants to share its voice.

I sit here beside the world's largest lake in the middle of Siberia in the early days of the 21st century but although I am lucky to be even alive to comprehend such moments, there is a sadness within me as a human being because as each day passes and my learned experience heightens the world we call home is exposed to me layer by layer and what I see does not have any meaning.

There are many questions that have been building up within me since I was a very young boy and it is only through the passing years and with an increase in wisdom that such questions can now be understood by me. The first question that I have is why does the human species have the ability from birth to destroy ourselves? This is a fact that is unconscionable to me and has no meaning for us as a living species. The fact remains that from the moment of my birth; it is ingrained within and upon me that I, a human being, can, if I choose to do so, take the life of another human being. Why would such a corrupted state be naturally passed on from one human to another without a say from that human being?

We are told that when a baby is born, it is pure and innocent but surely, this is a complete fallacy. The baby who is born is delicate and not yet developed but if it were truly born in a perfect state, then it would never grow up to hurt another human being. Our grand earth would fill a million times over with the amount of human beings who were born as delicate babies and who grew up to be barbaric murderers of other human beings.

We should not feel any way special because this corrupted state travels across all living species within the animal, plant and at the microbial level. Was such a decisive action pre-planned before the dawn of humankind and if so, for what reason of purity could be attached to the impurity of our own births? Are we all just part of a game fought over between two superpowers, that of the good and that of the bad? We are born into the light and we fade into the darkness and really, is the meaning of life a continuous battle between the light and the dark?

When I was a boy, I would play outside during the summer months of our school holidays but when darkness drew near I was called in by my parents and would often be told not to go out during the darkness because the bogey man would catch me. We are instinctively drawn towards the light because in the light we feel secure but when the sun sets and darkness enters the internal world of our own homes, this darkness scares us and removes our sense of security.

There is nothing to fear from darkness itself because all that is darkness is the removal of light when the sun sets. When the sun sets in one land, it rises in another so we always have the light and always have the darkness. It is not the darkness that we should be fearful of because the empty and the nothingness cannot harm us. There is one thing that can harm us and it reflects back into us when we look at our own reflection in the mirror.

Could it be the fact that before the human species walked this earth that it was decided that within each human being there would be the good and then there would also be the bad which would allow equilibrium in each person? If there is a grand design and creator of life, then perhaps there are two creators who fight side by side and watch over the Earth and its people as they battle continuously for each team. Therein lies the mystery within each person because how do we ever know what team we are part of?

I grew up in a home where my parents loved and protected me. They taught me the difference between right and wrong. As a young boy, I was part of the Catholic Church and I learned about the Old and New Testaments. Everything was chaotic in the Old Testament. Life was arbitrary and brutal in nature and in execution but then a young man came into the New Testament and brought with him a message of love and forgiveness. I learned about the Ten Commandments and how we all have a conscience that informs us at any time about right and wrong.

That same Catholic Church that I was part of and revered was externally preaching about love whilst internally they were abusing, raping and murdering babies, children and adults. Everything I was taught to be pure and true was impure and false. The Catholic Church became in its actions symbolic of the fight between the light and the dark; between all that is good and all that is bad.

That same baby who was born pure from its mother's womb grows into a boy and has the ability imprinted within itself to become a bully in the schoolyard against other children. The bully is insecure but realises very quickly that by going on the offensive that he can be dominant against the sensitive, the quiet, the gentle, the different and the submissive. Nobody had to teach the bully how to behave in this manner because such behaviours are born within us.

Each one of us, no matter who we are, has the potential to love but also the free will to hate. I can choose to be a good, moral and upright human being but if somebody breaks into my home and inflicts suffering onto my mother, then I can freely choose to take the life of the perpetrator. As a result, I too become a perpetrator and a person who tastes the bad. If I am walking along a street minding my own business and I witness a crime inflicted by one human onto another, I can choose to ignore and walk away from such an incident or I can choose to help the person who is being attacked. How do I know who is the good and who is the bad in that situation? Will my conscience inform me who I must support? If I do help the good by causing pain onto the bad, then surely I too become part of the bad because I choose to inflict such pain on another.

I was born in the latter part of the 20th century before the new millennium began. As a baby and young boy, I knew nothing of the crimes perpetrated by humans onto other humans during the many centuries before my birth. How much blood was spilled on the earth since the very first humans walked on its ground? If there was a message latent within our species, then surely over millennia we would have learned from, grasped onto and forged out a meaning to our existence whereby we choose to be good over to be bad.

At school, I learned all about the many military battles whereby one army invaded another but the end was always the same in that lifeless and decapitated bodies were scattered like eggshells across never-ending plains as their blood poured outward to witness not only the defeat of an army but the defeat of humans at the hands of other humans. We learned at school why the battle took place, who invaded the other so that we could equate the invader as the bad and the invaded as the good.

Finally, we learned the results of such a battle. Such results were always the same in that hundreds of lives were lost there and thousands of lives were lost here. I ask you now in the silence of Lake Baikal what was the meaning of such battles inflicted by man onto man?

Has the earth ever witnessed a peace since the arrival of man thousands of years ago? Even before the arrival of man, we know that millions of years ago, the dinosaurs roamed this earth we now call home. It was a different Earth then but it was their home and their lives were in many ways as chaotic and as brutal as the lives of humankind that followed them. The dinosaurs were earth's superior species but still they fought a war within themselves because their dominance knew no bounds. They were also born into a corrupted living state and nothing they did could alter such a state. They could not rise out of that dominant state into one of life and acceptance because their birth and inheritance did not allow such a metamorphosis. We, as human beings, inherited the land that the dinosaurs left behind and our birth was fated due to their untimely demise. We did not share a DNA structure with the dinosaurs but our short life thus far has proven that we have been just as brutal and as calculating as our predecessors.

Who were the first human beings to arrive on this Earth we call home? Are we to accept the position of the Old Testament and its first book Genesis where it posits that God created the first man and named him Adam and this followed the creation of a woman as company for the man? She was fashioned from the rib of man and was named Eve. How do we know that this actually happened and is a true assessment of the history of man due to the dysfunctional nature of man and its relationship with each other?

The naturalist Charles Darwin did not believe in a higher power creating humankind. He instead looked to evolution as the secret to holding man's original birth. The idea of human beings evolving in a survivor of the fittest scenario carries more logic because it certainly could explain the forces of darkness that pervade our species along with the forces for good. If we were fashioned to live by an all-knowing and all-powerful creator, then is such a creator one of purity or flawed?

A human being who creates another human being is essentially a flawed union because that flawed human being has traced its corrupted state all the way back to the first man who entered this earth. Therefore, if we are flawed as a species, then is not a creator if one exists also flawed? Why would a potential and all-knowing and all loving creator fashion a flawed species onto our planet?

There is, of course, another scenario which equally could be one of logic. If indeed there is an omnipresent and omnipotent creator, then is it possible that the great nemesis of love, which is death and the opposing force of good, which is evil could stand in opposition to this all loving creator?

The Bible tells us that this opposing force of good was once an angel of God but had designs of its own kingdom and so became a fallen angel and since that moment this force of evil has plagued the earth and will not stop until it takes as many human lives with it to the other side. There is, of course, a flaw with such a scenario in that the once good angel also had forces of corruption within and therefore such a corrupted state was there at its inception. The force of evil who was once an angel is believable for human beings because we can recognise such a corrupted state within ourselves.

What then of the all-knowing and all loving creator? Where was its creation manifested and how did it come into existence? Was such a creator manifested in the universe billions of years ago as the stars in the infinite space collided and waged a war to create a light?

Our universe is also endless and it is one of great magnificence coupled with an explosion of fire, one of superlative light and one caught in the depths of the abyss. Is it so then than just two questions remain unanswered and unsolved? Was the universe created with a massive explosion and out of this light, heat and energy came our solar system—the milky way with its life giving sun to heat the planets and, of course, our blue planet Earth that we call home?

If such a scenario did unfold millions of years ago, then perhaps Darwin was correct that human beings were created through the process of evolution. On the other hand, the second question also needs to be explored in depth. When the universe exploded, could it have created such an energy that it fashioned from infinite space a being that was to become all-knowing, all-loving and a creator of everything that was to exist, exists now and will exist until the end days?

We as human beings have never been able to extrapolate an answer to any of these questions. When parents give birth to their child, they raise that child and eventually the child becomes aware of who it is and where it came from. It has a right to know and understand its own existence.

As human beings, we do know about our past but no human being is aware of the exact truth of the existence of original life from our universe. We essentially come into this world in blind darkness and when we do eventually enter the light, it is a light filled with endless concealments. No human being has ever asked or demanded to be born. We have no say with regard to our conception and birth. We are conceived by chance and nothing is ever certain as our father's sperm fuses with our mother's egg with the intention of creating a life thereafter. The creation of life is filled with such uncertainty.

Due to the corrupt nature of our state the growing embryo is on a journey to life but ironically its main stumbling block comes from its own creator, human beings and due to our destructive forces the womb can be potentially an environment that hinders and eventually prevents the foetus from developing and making its way into the light.

I have often heard how life is all part of one grand plan and everything that happens was fated to do so. I abhor such simplistic statements because there is no logic attached to them. If everything was part of a grand plan, then why is a baby aborted from its mother's womb before entering the light? Why do millions of people all over our planet struggle to survive due to hunger and malnourishment? Why do human beings create and manufacture weapons of such ferocity that destroy our own species? Why does capital punishment exist in many parts of the world whereby we decide to take the life of a human being in revenge for the life that such a perpetrator committed onto another human being? Where is the grand plan when a mother is raped and brutally murdered in her own home, witnessed by her children? Where is the grand plan whereby one nation attacks another nation with explosive bombs ripping through the homes of the innocent families and children? Where is the grand plan that sees disease, deformities enter and utterly alter the life and the potential for such a being? Where is the grand plan that sees human blood spilled on the battlefield since man first entered this earth? If there is such a grandiose plan for our existence, we as human beings have not learned about it or witnessed such a plan. We continue to live amongst the havoc with the senseless.

Returning to my initial question as to why human beings have the ability from birth to destroy one another? This is surely the crux and central point of the flaw within humanity. Human beings since they walked out from their caves as the first humans knew then that our great nemesis is our fellow humans, which includes our own families.

For thousands of years of recorded history, man has been shown to be destructive against one another. We have never been united because it was fated that we would be divisive for one another. We are all shocked when we learn about another invasion of a land by the aggressor but internally this is our inheritance by virtue of our birth into our home. We have never known the earth to be at full peace. There could be peace on many lands but on one land there could exist unmitigated destruction of a people by another people.

Throughout history there have been multiple empires which were formed with the intention of forging a war for land across space within our earth. The results were always the same: a colossal loss of life, a destruction of cultures as the aggressor stole new territory for its own self-interest and lust for power. We recall from history the dynasties of China, the caliphates of the Middle East, the ironically named holy Roman Empire that was anything but holy as it ravaged through lands and destroyed people for over a thousand years.

The empires went on with the Mali Empire, the Burmese Empire, the Ethiopian Empire, the Swedish Empire, the Inca Empire, the Nanda Empire, the Gupta Empire, the Hunnic Empire, the Dutch Empire, Kievan Rus Empire, the Kushan Empire, the Belgian Empire, the Parthian Empire, the Byzantine Empire, the Italian Empire, the Mughal Empire, the Tibetan Empire, Nazi Germany, the Ottoman Empire, the Mexican Empire, the Macedonian Empire, the Empire of

Japan, the Portuguese Empire, the French Empire, the Spanish Empire, the Persian Empire, the Russian Empire, the Mongol Empire, the British Empire.

No land, territory or peoples were free from such a ravaging campaign formed by power hungry leaders who led armies out into battle to take the lands of others in order to claim such lands as their own. These were human beings who were all born solely dependent into the world from the warmth of their mother's womb and yet in their millions as men became beasts on horses with their weapons at hand in order to destroy their enemies.

So I ask once again, why were the human species allowed from birth to be able to destroy one another? How many human lives have been taken due to the evil acts of empires forging their wars for territory and peoples? Are all of those lives that were taken in a brutal manner in their billions accounted for? What was the meaning and justification for such acts of brutality from one empire to another? Has human beings essentially been used in a dirty war between the forces of good and the forces of evil? Was it the fate of humanity that man would wage a never-ending war on itself? Surely, the face and geography of the world has been irreparably altered forever. Each empire was born, forged a path of destruction, was then defeated, replaced and the never-ending cycle begins once more until we arrive into the 21st century.

Is there a connection between the force of good versus the force of evil when it comes to how religion has been examined and lived throughout history? A persons religious choice evolves by mere chance by way of their own birth. Take, for example, I who was born in Ireland within the continent of Europe. It was more than likely that I would be introduced to Christianity and raised as a Christian due to strong Christian roots developed over two millennia from Jerusalem and north into Europe.

However, had I been born in India exactly at the same time of my birth, then it would be more than likely that I would have been introduced to Hinduism and consequently raised as a Hindu devotee. If I had been born in Thailand, then perhaps I would have been introduced and raised as a Buddhist.

Alternatively, if I had been born in the Middle East or northern Africa, then I would probably have been introduced to Islam and raised as a Muslim following the Prophet Muhammad and worshipping Allah. It was also possible that I could have been born within the state of Israel and then I would have been introduced to Judaism and raised a Jewish man.

History has shown us that one's religion has a very real and decisive impact on how we live our lives. History has also revealed to us how one's religion can have a very divisive outcome in their lives because instead of two human beings coming together in a manner of cultural integration and peace it has been found that their own birth religions can be a real stumbling block in uniting such cultures and often in the end these two different religious identities go in separate directions never to co-exist again. If humans have been born into a corrupted state of being, then it is logical that the religion they choose to follow has also been corrupted.

There is no perfect state of a human being so when such a corrupted being is born into a religious way of life, they don't question that life because it came from within their own family, community, country and culture so as a result it is very real and truthful to them. Their whole identity was created and becomes formed within such a religion and they will love and honour such a way of life because that is what they were taught as real and truthful.

It is also logical that a monotheistic religious follower will by a process of elimination begin to be taught how their religion and their God is the real truth and creator of this world but the other religions have a similar belief structure so the question is which religion reveals truth?

Of all religions, it is Hinduism that is the oldest, originating over three thousand years before the birth of Christ and beginning along the Indus Valley and connecting with the Aryan culture. It has survived from generation to generation for 5000 years and onward it goes as it rejects the Judaic, Christian and Islamic belief system that there is only one path for the follower of Hinduism to gain enlightenment and reaching the divine state.

It spread from the Aryan culture with the sacred Veda text and connected with classical Hinduism whereby in order for the person to reach a true enlightened state that person must transmigrate from their own body by way of reincarnation which is determined by karma and how their previous birth will impact on their next birth. The person must gain true wisdom and reach a unity with their own soul.

It is the one religion where there is a deep connection between the masculine and the feminine. There are many gods and goddesses and the soul will have many reincarnations so it is therefore possible that the soul will be masculine and feminine during its many births along the cycle of life to the divine.

There is a deep philosophical tradition within Hinduism because the belief of all Hindus is that the human can become divine by a way of life that exudes outward from the soul in a lived process of action, duty, prayer and wisdom. The Hindu devotee is always looking ahead to the next birth but whilst at the same time they must perform their duties during this birth to allow a safe karma to exist in order to transmigrate safely into the next birth.

There is a deep spirituality at the death of all Hindus because they return to the waters of their birth and the burning of their flesh into ashes connects from one birth into the next birth. The Earth and its water always forms the backdrop for such ritual because the transmigration must occur in the correct manner into the next birth.

Hinduism and India have witnessed attacks on its culture and spiritual way of life from both Islam and Christianity. The attack of Christianity into India came by way of British colonialism, which expanded and divided India and their culture. The eventual departure of the British divided India and brought two new states in Pakistan and Bangladesh. These two states were where Islam increased a teleological divide between Islam and Hinduism, which resulted in widespread violence and loss of life across the subcontinent.

The criticism I have with Hinduism is not with their belief in a reach for a state of enlightenment and the divine. It is with their ancient hereditary and hierarchal caste system because this system is deeply flawed, unequal and not divine centred. It works well for the priests and scholars of the highest caste— the Brahmin but it is a form of degradation and utter misery for the lower caste the Shudras and below the Shudras are what is called the untouchables or Dalits whereby they are seen as impure and dirty and can never come out from the bottom of their caste into a hierarchal level.

The caste system may be outlawed today in India but vestiges of its belief system remain and it continues to form a stumbling block for poorer Hindus who live along the margins of society. What would the Veda, Bhagavad Gita and Upanishads sacred texts say about how such lower caste Hindus can find equality within their lifetimes and how they can reach enlightenment in order to become divine?

If this ancient religion began with God, the all-powerful, it was certainly passed onto corrupted and flawed human beings, which slowly changed the belief structure and divided their devotees into an unequal structure that was certainly not inspired by the divine.

Judaism, another ancient religion can trace its origins thousands of years and a belief system in one God who gave them their ancient text, the Tanakh on which to follow their supreme God through a series of decalogues and a way of life consisting of following the Torah, worshipping their God and on good deeds and love. The Jews believe that they are God's chosen people, as it was a promise made by God to Abraham that he will return them to Israel.

Everything in Judaism and the belief of all Jews is that God exists and that God is eternal. Jews cannot believe in any other Gods or idols because it runs contradictory to their faith in one God only. Their sacred text, the Torah, is divine because it holds the words of God. Jews also believe that God sees all their deeds, both good and bad. Jews are told that one day a Messiah will come to bring them home and that on death, they will be resurrected as a promise by God.

Like all religions, Judaism believes that their followers have free will in this life but with free will comes much responsibility through prayer in order to be rewarded in heaven for their good lives here on Earth. On the other hand, bad deeds will not go unnoticed and a form of punishment and retribution exists for the follower of God.

Throughout history, this ancient religion has been persecuted and sacked from their homeland by first the Assyrian Empire and later the Babylonian Empire, which demolished their holy temple and sent the Jews into exile once again. Later, it was the turn of the brutal Roman Empire that destroyed their holy temple and another exile awaited the Jews across the Middle East and north Africa. The most devastating attack on Judaism and its people was during the Holocaust in Europe, where it was decided as part of a Final Solution to exterminate all Jews from Europe. They were first murdered in mass shootings and later millions of Jews were sent into ghettos and onto concentration and extermination camps, where they were systematically murdered through a process of enslavement, starvation and then gassing them to death in large numbers. The callous Nazis tried to conceal their crimes by burning the Jewish bodies and incinerating them into mere ashes. Such a degradation of the Jewish bodies is forbidden in Judaism as on death the Jewish deceased must be buried in the corrupt physical state that it is in before making its resurrected journey to be with God.

Could it have been the life of Jesus who was predicted to be the coming Messiah that was born into and raised Jewish but who was crucified for bringing a new way of life that was contrary to the traditions of Judaism? How has the crucifixion of Jesus and his reported resurrection affected Judaism as it is practiced today?

There is an integral goodness in the traditions of Judaism but like all religions, it has become strained because of how human beings have affected such traditions. Has it been that Judaism will always go through persecutions for its belief in one all loving and powerful God? There is also a continuous strain in the relationship between Israel and Palestine as they fight to claim ownership of a strip of physical land beside the Mediterranean Sea. Such a strain is rooted in religious beliefs in that Judaism in Israel versus Islam in Palestine. Therein lies the corruption within both religions because each of their followers are not following a loving God anymore because that God that they follow would want each of these two states to cease fighting and become brothers and sisters under God's union. Both states have long since denied a loving God and followed a path of destruction.

Of all the main religions it is Buddhism that does not worship a supreme God. Buddhism began with a human being named Siddhartha Gautama in India as he sat under a tree to contemplate on his existence, his suffering and an acceptance of his life before reincarnation into the next birth. There are no pre-set rules guided by an all-powerful God for its devotees to follow. There is no God watching onto see our good deeds and bad transgressions. Buddhism is the transformation of the human being to become a good and whole person who seek wisdom and a desire to love all living things on this Earth. It is a way of life that any human being can look to and become part of because at the heart of Buddhism is suffering. All human beings, no matter where we come from, understand suffering and how such suffering is unavoidable in this life. Buddhism teaches us that when we accept that this life is one of impermanence and suffering, then we can begin to look inward to our soul and begin a process of wisdom, liberation and peace. There is no place for strong desires and conflicts within Buddhism. Buddhism tries to slowly eradicate the corruption that is innate to all human lives.

Buddhism and Hinduism have many connections in that there is a complete union of the masculine with the feminine in each person. Throughout cultures in our world, the masculine male is always seen as different to the feminine female. The masculine is strong and protective whereas the feminine is submissive and nurturing. Our world allows the two genders to work side by side but within Buddhism and Hinduism the human state is genderless where both the masculine and feminine resides in the body and both genders allow the person to become more enlightened, more free and at peace with oneself.

Buddhism is a religion of peace because there is no supreme God in which to fight for in order to hold on to traditional beliefs and rules. If an atheist considered becoming Hindu, Jewish, Christian or Muslim, that would entail many rules and rituals to abide by, whereas Buddhism is more adaptable to any human being because it is always human centred. Buddhism is more about listening to the inner voice whereas the God centred religions focus on the external prayerful duties.

The Buddhist monk rests in silence and waits in order to be moved into a state of enlightenment whereby this life is seen as a journey into a re-birth. For me, as an observer, I see Buddhism as the least divisive and most compassionate of all the main religions. Buddhism does not need to defend itself in argument. It simply remains silent and waits to be moved from within its soul. Buddhists do not need to form armies and attack other lands because it is a religion of peace. There is no message from any supreme being. The message is to accept our natural state of existence.

If there is a criticism of Buddhism, perhaps the only one I can offer up is that how do we know that on our deaths that we will transmigrate into another body to begin a cycle of life once more?

One religion tells us that upon death we will be resurrected to be with God whilst another religion tells us that on death we will return to the earth through a process of reincarnation. Nothing is ever certain and nobody holds all the truth due to the corruptive natural state of our beings. All we can do is to move onward and search for this ultimate truth for our existence. The only truth that we can trust during life is the truth that exists within ourselves. We exist and we live and they are the truths that we must live by.

Islam, like Judaism and Christianity, holds the belief that there is one true and all loving and powerful God and that the revelation of God has been passed onto the Prophet Muhammad, who is the living teacher of God's holy message, the Quran. The Quran is a message of love, compassion and a justice with a belief in God who will judge all his people on death.

Of all religions, Islam spread the fastest following the death of the Prophet Muhammad. All Muslims must follow the five pillars of wisdom that incorporate a belief in one God that is Allah, a practice of praying five times each day, a compulsory practice of giving to the needy where the emphasis is on compassion, a focus on fasting one's body during the holy month of Ramadan and finally a visit to Mecca if possible at least once in their life where all Muslims converge to their holy place of worship.

At the heart of Islam are the forces of Islamic law (Shariah Law) that determines its practices and Islamic Sufism that focus on spirituality and a mystic connection between the Muslim followers, Muhammad the messenger and Allah the supreme God. Islam experienced a golden age following the death of Muhammad and its empires spread and flourished across the Middle East and north Africa.

Islam is a religion of political conquests and such conquests are unavoidable when discussing Islam. Islamic conquests began in Arabia and went north across Persia. Their whole aim was an expansion of territory. The Arabs conquered the Persian Empire entirely and the Byzantine Empire lost Damascus. War and plundering of land was the aim of the Islamic conquests.

There was an energy to conquest from the desserts of Arabia in order to gain new lands for its own. The Arabs consolidated vast swathes of land and increased their wealth through civilisations. The great tragedy of Islam is that at its core is a message of temperance, submission and a hope that one day the Muslim follower will be reunited with their God.

Islam has all the ingredients necessary to follow through with such a message but again it is a religion of corrupted human beings who made decisions at its birth to conquer, plunder, destroy with a hunger and desire for power over love for Allah. If their great and all loving God Allah was to return, what message would he give to his followers in the 21st century in recognition of the over 1500 years of life since the death of their Prophet Muhammad? Has every Muslim faithfully followed the five pillars of Islam?

The history of Islam has shown a lust for power that is not compatible with the eternal values of Islam and the message of Allah. Islam gained so much land, wealth, wisdom but at what cost has it lost its soul?

The comparison between Buddhism and Islam is like a comparison of the many facets that make up our own self. Buddhism is a religion of the quiet and a quest to conquer its desire and live a life accepting one's own suffering, whereas Islam's fall was its exterior need for power. If Islam was a like a house, its foundations would be very solid, as it holds the tools to build a home worthy of its master. However, when an external desire to conquer for power ignited the soul of Muslims, then the home and structure grew up and became a distortion to the imagined home of their master. If there is any hope for Islam, then it must rid itself of the desire for power through political systems and return to a balance between the external Shariah Law and an internal need for Sufism in order to listen to the message of Allah. Furthermore, there should be a full union between Sunni and Shia Muslims because they are all disciples of Allah and only through such a union can they progress as one Islam.

Christianity is the most tragic and contradictory of all religions. Its birth was one of extraordinary love, submission to the father and a true sacrifice demanding nothing in return. The difference between Christianity and other religions is that God came onto the Earth as a human being through his son Jesus Christ and through God, Jesus Christ and the spirit they formed a unity in which to spread a message of love and of hope for all peoples on the Earth.

There was no law but a following of a man who believed in what he preached and showed through him a message of forgiveness, repentance and a willingness to begin once more to try and love. He only lived on Earth for 33 years and thirty of those years were unrevealed. The final three years have left an indelible mark on our Earth.

There is something so uncontradictory about the life of Jesus. He was a leader but not a king that wore a crown. He was Jewish and faithfully followed the practices of Judaism but he brought a new message to the world which was one of peace and a desire to love each person as we love oneself. The message of Jesus was one of the internal love of the individual radiating outward to love everything externally.

Our whole system of time and date follows with the birth of Jesus (BC) and (AD) (Anno Domini) the year of our lord. The life and death of Jesus is a microcosm of the life and death of humanity. Jesus, through his message of peace, showed the goodness and the light within humanity. His murder through a public hanging by the Romans signifies the opposing force of evil hidden within the darkness of man. The real significance of Christianity and the life of Jesus was an empty tomb found following his crucifixion. If indeed Jesus was the son of God as he proclaimed and rose from the dead on the third day, then his message must live on through his followers.

The criticism of Christianity is how divided it has always been since the departure of its leader. How can Christianity unite with other religions when it is deeply disjointed from within? The Catholic and Orthodox facets of Christianity are deeply divided in terms of their moral leader on earth and equally the Catholic and Protestant churches have had a decisive split over rules and governance.

The Great Schism between the Catholic and Orthodox Church took place in the 11th century and the Protestant Reformation dates to the 16th century. The meaning and goodness of Christianity rests with its founder and moral leader Jesus but ever since his untimely departure an illness through the corruption and continued darkness within has divided this once pure religion into impurity. Could it be that the darkness and opposing forces of the bad which brought an end to the natural life of Jesus as a human being has infiltrated this once religion of love into a religion of a loss of self and nothingness?

There have been many good and submissive Christians throughout history who faithfully followed the teachings of their master but equally there has been a cancer from the very moment of the departure of Jesus from the Earth. Christianity's descent into evil and the boundaries of hell became real during the dark ages of the crusades formed against their enemy Islam. The great folly of such crusades was that each religion was following their one true God, who proclaimed peace and love through its followers and yet they battled to murder such enemies that were seen as children of God to their leaders. The crusades brought the death of the innocence of love.

The destructive force within all religions is the very people who proclaim and follow such religions, mankind. I can understand why a person chooses to be an atheist in this world, because why would anybody follow a religion that is deeply flawed because of ourselves?

There is, of course, much to admire within religions as they do bring large gatherings of people together to observe rituals and follow with a desire to love. However, we cannot alter our stain, which has been present from our births. We can try to be good and to live faithful lives but even if one person chooses to be bad, then it creates a domino effect whereby all of its people are infected with such darkness.

The most silent of the religions is Buddhism and ironically this is the one religion that is without a God. It focuses on the need for mankind to change itself from within and to accept our life of suffering before we depart this world. Could it be that the world needs to eradicate ourselves from the religious lives we knew and practiced for a new way of living?

Religions and a religious way of life have been with humanity for some 5000 years and whilst there has been so much good come from a copious amount of practices, there has also been tremendous suffering caused by the perpetrators of such a religious way of life. We can follow one religion but then we are automatically divided from another. Each religion claims to hold the truth, especially the God like religions. Can everybody be right or perhaps we are all wrong and living a complete lie?

As human beings, we have destructive forces of good and bad running through our bodies and so we bring both the good and the bad to such religions. The Buddha's message was sincere because he worked on the internal mechanism of himself alone so that he could become a better person than he once was. There is a need for each one of us to become silent and go into the quietness of our world so that we can ponder on our existence and how we can become a better person within the light.

As long as we have a multitude of religions in our world, we will remain divided as a human species. The true virtue of a religious life is to bring people together and unite but tragically, the many religions that are practiced here on earth has the opposite effect. When we are faithful to one way of life, we ignore and often degrade another way of life. This is a deep flaw within our humanity.

We must first conquer the darkness within our own soul before we can emerge into the light. As long as we remain in the darkness, our world will continue to be divided and man will continue to suffer at the hands of one another. This is our death drive. Our religion and religious way of life is mostly chosen by our culture, geography and our birth family. It is all by chance and we have relatively little say in it.

In order to become more rounded as a species, we could whilst been part of one religion, begin to investigate the other religions as a way to unite in compassion for our brothers and sisters. We should live a life like the Buddha's because he always considered the lives of others before committing on his own journey. By reaching within our own soul, we can begin to see who we truly are and consequently we can begin to live a life that is more concerned with the light than it is with the dark.

Chapter 11
Fragments of Death

The human species' ability to destroy itself has not waned with the passing of time. In fact, it has intensified and as each generation fades into the next and a culmination of centuries and millennia follows each human being and the culture of people inherits the destruction and stain from the previous generation.

My life, culture and peoples have inherited the damning inditements of the 20th century that concluded a millennium and century with a barbaric onslaught of evil perpetrated by human beings onto human beings. It was the century of death. Death permeated all facets of the 20th century. Individual cultures forged into empires and the results were two bloody world wars that brought human depravity locally into universal death. It began in darkness within the trenches of the First World War and lasted for four years with a death toll of twenty million. When it finally ended in 1918 with an armistice on 11 November, they said then that it was the war to have ended all wars.

However, as human beings have continuously caused destruction throughout its life, it was surely inevitable that more violence and war would follow. A mere twenty-one years later came a Second World War and it was more calculating, strategic with an emphasis on a great Germanic empire forced onto the peoples of Europe for six long and death filled years. The true evil within the darkness of humanity was unleashed by the megalomania of Adolf Hitler as his hatred towards the Jews of Europe had no limits.

Each generation and century is shocked by the actions of the previous generation and the horrific crimes that were enacted onto the Jews and other peoples who were seen as undesirable brought to the attention of the world a systematic cleansing of such a culture and people in the concentration and extermination camps throughout Europe.

It is not only Hinduism that has a history of a caste system. The Nazis had their own caste system too with the Aryans at the top of the pyramid and at the very bottom were the Jews who were seen like mere animals to be dealt with in any manner that the dominant Nazis chose to inflict on their submissive subjects. Each generation inherits the previous generation. Was that the case for Adolf Hitler and could he have been inspired by the Armenian massacre in 1915, where approximately one million Armenians were brutally massacred by the Ottoman Empire?

There was no world response to that massacre and the world's first global genocide inflicted onto a people. Over a century later and still the once Ottoman Empire and now Turkey refuses to accept and acknowledge their actions onto innocent Armenians. Perhaps the failure of a world response inspired Hitler as his hatred of the Jews increased when he took power in 1933. What were the crimes of the Jews, the Roma, the Jehovah's Witnesses, the homosexuals, the physically and mentally deformed? To the Nazis, they were not Aryan and so were not even classed as human beings. The Nazis rounded up these undesirables, herded them into ghetto's then transported them to factories of death where they were gassed to death, their emaciated bodies starving for nourishment were then burnt in ovens and finally the evil completed with the dumping of ashes into large pits.

I remember visiting the former home of Anne Frank where she and her family went into hiding before they were captured by the Nazis and sent first to Auschwitz and later to Bergen Belsen where Anne and her sister Margot succumbed to typhus. Their former home is a museum now and a place of witness because it is a record of how Jewish people were petrified for their lives due to an attacking enemy that would not stop until all traces of Judaism were removed from Europe. I remember looking at photos of young Anne with her family during happier times. She loved to write in her diary and words on a page were very real and important for her. They formed a creative external response to the internal dilemma that she and her family faced during self-imprisonment. She died as a teenager as illness devoured her body within the gates of hell at Bergen Belsen concentration camp. Her life was just as important and real as every other life during the Holocaust and yet it passed quickly in the shadows of the deathly camps.

The Jews of Europe and the world may rightfully ask God about their once covenant with him and where was God when their ailing and bone protruding bodies entered the gas chambers of the death camps. If God was not present there, then perhaps his nemesis the prince of darkness was present as his slaves of Adolf Hitler, Adolf Eichmann and Josef Mengele unleashed their terror onto the innocents.

Could it be that the two defining images from the evil 20th century were that of the innocent babies screaming for their lives as murder knocked upon their hearts and the mushroom cloud of poisonous heat and radiation filled the skies over Hiroshima and Nagasaki as the world's first atomic bomb was fired by the United States onto the Japanese Empire as revenge for the empires attack at Pearl Harbour? History has forever recorded who created, planned and ignited the world's first atomic bomb. This is yet another example of how man continues to conjure up new and more crushing attacks on his fellow man so that the enemy will be annihilated. How many innocent lives were cruelly taken on that fateful day as little boy hit the earth on Hiroshima and later on Nagasaki? How much time, money and energy were spent in strategically planning such an assault on the enemy? The lives that were instantly incinerated and vapourised on that day are forever shadows in the nightly terror dreams of the attackers.

If World War 1 was supposed to have been the war to have ended all wars, then the firing of the atomic bomb onto Japan was probably the defining moment of a brutal war and century. However, lessons have not been learned. Wisdom has not yet reached to the sincere soul of humankind. When human beings commit such crimes onto other human beings, these events can never be taken back as the loss of life cannot physically come out from their graves, their ashes and their own shadows.

I was not yet born when such events happened but when I did enter this world, I am forever an inheritor of the death camps of Europe and the atomic bomb hitting Japan. My own generation all over the world inherited such events from history. We have listened to the many commentaries and political leaders discussing endlessly how we must create a lasting peace and still conflicts rage on throughout our world because nobody questions man's own conflict within itself.

If there is a grand and all-encompassing creator out there, then why does such suffering continue to consume our world and our peoples? Could it be that the dark forces within humanity have been unleashed and the good forces become impotent when faced with such ferocity? A person who walks the path of peace and is morally good is never on an offensive path, whereas the person who walks the path of wickedness and evil will always go on the strategic offensive in order to nullify the passive moralist.

So, what can the good people and moral citizens of this planet do in order to stop such evil? We can certainly make a moral stand internally by refusing to allow the darkness to enter us but what if that vileness and immoral structures are ingrained onto both our country and our peoples? What if the sickness of evil will spread like an incurable cancer just like it did in Nazi Germany? Are we foolish or naïve enough to believe that if we had lived under such an evil regime that we would not have tasted blood too from our victims? If we are consciously aware, that evil is carried out but do nothing in return, then both our silence and apathy is defining our character as part of the dark forces too.

In the end, we either choose the light or the dark. We cannot exist in both worlds. If we reside in the light, then we have a responsibility to ensure the light continues to shine but if we open the door to the darkness, then it will close behind us and the light will forever depart our soul.

Peace did not enter the world in 1945 with the defeat of Nazi tyranny but the ideological regimes of communism which first spread from the Soviet Union at the beginning of the Russian Revolution spread quickly with the rise to power of Josef Stalin and his depraved assault onto millions of his own people as they were banished to the gulags of Siberia. Stalin was the great leader and hero for all Soviet people as he prevented the evil regime of Nazism to conquer their lands and culture.

Who could have predicted that the hero of the allies in the Great Patriotic War would turn in on his own people and create mass graves across the Russian landscape? It was inconceivable and yet once again, the dark forces within man reigned supreme on his passive subjects. When we reflect on the evil in the 20th century, it was the cruel undertakings of both Hitler and Stalin that will be recalled and both dark forces will forever be placed side by side as examples of the worst in us as human beings.

We can only ask why would human beings treat other human beings in such ways but the answer to such questions is no longer a mystery and surprise for us anymore. The longer we live, the more that humanity is slowly extinguishing out from us. When we are born, there is a tenderness and an innocence as everything to us is new and a sensation. As time moves on and we grow, we experience a different life and one that is filled with the best and the worst of humanity. This is when the light is switched on and yet the darkness remains.

Along with Nazism, the equally depraved communism with its lies and propaganda destroyed Russia and quickly spread like a contagious virus into China. It was the age of Mao Zedong and yet another force of darkness spread through China, which resulted in a Cultural Revolution whereby an entire generation of Chinese people were starved to death in the collective farms throughout Chinese lands.

China who once kept a watchful eye over their evil neighbour the Japanese Empire was blinded to the evil that resided within their own land. As human beings, our natural instinct is to always protect ourselves from any form of attack but how can we prevent an attack that begins within where we are blinded to its beginnings and powerless to its destructive effects?

From China, communism spread into Cambodia with the rise of Pol Pot, who became a shadowy figure as he slowly infiltrated his own lands and peoples with a desire for a return to their former and glorious Khmer past at its centre of Angkor. How could one man with an army of deranged followers expel their own people to the countryside, detain and torture them and send such people to their deaths within the killing fields? Instead of murdering their victims with guns and bullets, they decided to save on such weapons and arms by barbarically and slowly hacking their victims to death. A few years ago, I visited the S-21 Museum in Phnom Penh where the interrogation took place and then immediately afterward I went to the city of Choeung Ek some fifteen kilometres outside of Phnom Penh where the killing fields of Pol Pot's genocide took place. Under those fields were buried the bodies of innocent Cambodians into mass graves. Today more than 8000 skulls are arranged by sex and are visible inside seventeen clear glass panels high in a very poignant memorial where one enters by taking off one's shoes and remembering the lives that were taken on what is now sacred ground.

When remembering 20th century crimes, one cannot forget the tragedy of Vietnam as it tried to free itself from the colonial clutches of France and then Vietnam ended a bloody and long war that forever altered its people and culture. There is a museum in Ho Chi Minh city called the War Remnants Museum and that museum tells the full and honest truth of the Vietnam War. There are three distinct levels to that museum and it is floor two that is the most graphic as it depicts the human suffering as a result of the United States army using agent orange/dioxin for a civilian population during the Vietnam War. Many children were born later with birth defects. The Vietnamese nation brought a lawsuit against the United States for using a horrendous chemical on innocent people but they did not win the case. There is a quote at the War Remnants Museum taken from the American Declaration on Human Rights and how it states that all citizens of America have a right to the pursuit of happiness. What about the people of Vietnam? Aren't they entitled to the very same pursuit of happiness? It certainly was denied to them during the Vietnam War and it reached its most vile moment during the massacre of My Lai, where American troops rounded up men, women and children and murdered some five hundred of them. The allies of World War 2 became the aggressors of a war that was not their war or their lands or their peoples. They always maintained that they entered the Vietnam War with the intention of preventing the domino effect of communism spreading throughout Asia but when the Vietnam War ended, was such American interference and aggression justified?

Death in the 20th century kept its assault on humankind and towards the last days of the old millennium in Rwanda over the course of a mere one hundred days between April-July 1994 800,000 Tutsi civilians were brutally massacred by the Hutu majority. It was an intense propaganda campaign planned by the Hutu aggressors as they let loose the darkness from within onto their own people in acts of complete madness showing human beings how far we had descended from rational and empathetic humans to ones of a blood thirsty lust and a desire to rid ourselves of the light that we once possessed.

At Srebrenica in Bosnia in July 1995, Bosnian Muslims who had lived all their lives in Srebrenica and Potocari were rounded up by Bosnian Serbs because the Bosnian army wanted to create a racially pure Serbia. In the end, 8,000 young Bosnian men and boys were captured and murdered by Bosnian Serbs as the United Nations and the world looked on in silence. The dark forces within man were allowed to wield the axe of their terror and assault onto their victims. The forces for light and the truth walked away and hid their shame amongst the wallowing degradation of their own impotence. Once again, the darkness was dominant and on the offensive while the light was weak, submissive and without a soul.

Following World War 1, the world and its leaders promised that we would never return to violence again but then the Second World War came with the Holocaust. The world screamed never again but then we later witnessed violence in Palestine, Korea and then Vietnam. The world said no more but then came Cambodia and its killing fields, followed by Srebrenica and Rwanda. The world continued to say enough of violence but then at the beginning of the 21st century witnessed the attacks on the World Trade Centre in New York and the civil war in Syria that has torn a culture and a people apart. When will it all cease?

That is probably an easy question to answer as it will probably cease when human beings cease to live on this planet. We cannot blame anybody outside of our planet because we are the only aggressors here. We are the manufacturers, collaborators, instigators and executioners of all this violence. Where will such genocide strike next and who will be its victims? What has the 21st century learned from the evil crimes of the 20th century? That man hates itself!

That brings us here to our lives in the 21st century. We have inherited the life and the cultures before us but now it is our turn to determine what the next generations and century will inherit by our own actions and decisions during this century. We have learned much and gained a lot of wisdom from the evil carried out throughout the 20th century.

Is there a common cohesion for unity and a lasting peace or are the dark forces building up within us once again to be escalated into the world at some point in the future? The basic and fundamental right for all human beings on this planet is the right to a life. The tainted life within the body of each human is sacred and yet it is not our property to own for the very fact that we did not choose to be born and have life here on this planet. Due to such a fact, we take temporary guardianship of our bodies and lives as we forge out an identity in order to survive.

One of the most tragic realities of life anywhere today in our world is the law that allows for a growing life in its mother's womb to be aborted, murdered and for that life to be extinguished into nothingness thereby cleansing that potential life of its right to come into existence and live as a fully formed human being. There is a colour photo that rests within a frame and sits on my writing desk at home. It is a photo of a growing life within its mother's womb, surrounded by the amniotic sac. The baby rests still whilst going through their period of creation. The image shows the perfection of the human face as the baby sucks on the thumb of its left hand. This image of life brings enormous comfort to me and often if I feel down in some way I will sit in silence and dwell upon this image.

We now live in a world where it is acceptable for a woman at a certain stage during her pregnancy to terminate the life that grows within her. The father who also created this life has no say in such a decision. This decision is made by the mother because within her rests the growing life. I often hear the phrase, my life, my body being thrown about when it comes to contemplating abortion but this phrase contains no logic at all. Neither the mother or the father own this life growing inside the woman. The life of the growing baby is autonomous in that it is distinct from all other life on this planet. Therefore, nobody can claim ownership of that growing life. When we create a life, we do not own that life because we do not even own our own life. If we owned our own bodies and lives, then surely we would not relinquish life from our bodies and, consequently, death would never arrive for us. There is another way to prove that we do not own our bodies or the life we created. If we owned the growing life within the mother's womb, then surely we would have a right to take that life outside of the womb for the very illogical fact that we own such a life. However, we know that such an act would be criminal and one of murder onto the innocent life so that proves that the created life is a separate entity to its creators. The life of the unborn but developing baby is not owned by its creators. The parents created such a life but the growing child has full rights to live its life and eventually choose its own path in life. Furthermore, if it is wrong to take the life of the created life outside of the mother's womb, it is equally as wrong to take the life of the growing baby within the nine months before the child is born.

There is nothing elegant or pure about the word abortion. To abort literally means to bring to a premature end due to some fault or problem. When a growing life is aborted, we by our actions are inferring blame onto the growing life for its surprise existence, we blame the growing life for having some fault or physical problem or we blame the innocent life for having been created during the barbaric act of rape inflicted onto the innocent woman by her violator. The growing life did not choose to come into this world but when its existence becomes clear, then this potential life deserves the exact same rights as all living human beings and that is simply to live. The physical process of abortion is a barbarically criminal act done in the silence and in the shadows of hospitals and clinics. Abortions are performed by doctors which is the great oxymoron. In just one abortion, the performing doctor is breaking the Hippocratic Oath as it does cause harm and more by erasing the physical life of the potential child. Everything about a physical abortion is brutal. It is the direct attack on the unborn child inside by the dark forces of mankind outside with their weapons of death in hand.

After the doctor administers the anaesthetic, the vagina walls are opened in order to gain access. The cervix which is closed during pregnancy to protect the life of the child will be physically opened using metal rods called dilators. The doctor now has entered the uterus where the voiceless life rests. The growing life has a heartbeat, fingers, arms, legs but its bone formation is still developing so they are physically weak during this trimester period. The doctor then inserts a catheter suction which is plastic but firm. The merciless moment occurs when this powerful catheter is placed into the uterus of the mother and the precious life inside is powerfully and callously torn apart and the body tissue squeezes tightly into the catheter, where it follows on a journey down into the machine. The life of the nameless baby has died and forever, its once light within the womb has turned into darkness within the suction machine below. It is yet another example within humanity of the opposing forces of good versus evil.

If every potential life was aborted from its mother's womb, then life as we know it would cease to exist within our own generation. Abortion is a crime and we should not be afraid to state that. Abortion is the deliberate and forceful ending of an innocent life who cannot defend itself against its perpetrators. When pregnant women walked into the gas chambers of extermination camps during the Holocaust, each mother carried two lives; her own and the life of her unborn child. Each life was as precious and as sacred as the other. The gassing of her body and that of her unborn child was murder committed by the vile Nazis but what is the connection between the killing of the unborn child in the gas chambers of Europe and the abortion of the unborn life throughout the world? It is murder!

We have no comprehension of the nature and processes that take place as life is conceived, takes form, develops and is born into our world. The creation and developing of a life is a work of divinity that is witnessed but never fully grasped by humanity. The physical bodies that we dwell within were slowly and intricately developed as each day passed within our mother's womb. We have no recollection of such a moment but it was the most time-honoured period of our lives because without that period of slow and delicate growth we would not have a life that we live each day within this world. Everything about our development after a fusion of the sperm and egg is about the divine development of our own unique heart which allows us to breathe and live as we set out on a silent and dangerous journey towards the external life. Each part of the body is taking shape and if allowed, it will form into a full human being with its own unique personality. As the mother continues her journey externally, her unborn child is growing each day as the muscles and complex vertebrae systems connect and create. After a mere nine weeks following the fusion of the sperm with the egg, the embryo takes the shape and form of a small baby that we can instantly recognise because that tiny life was once you and I, a long time ago. The complexity of work going on within our cells is beyond human and yet the divine was created and lives within the human. Who is behind such divine work? Where do such innate complex structures be given form and be allowed to work through the corruptive human state? Is it you who is the great creator of all life? Are you the reason why we have a conscience, why we have autonomy and why we have the ability to love but also to hate? Is there an ultimate price on the head and within the heart of each human being and is death the final relinquishing of the corrupt and dark forces that reside within us? Is it you that our eyes will finally rest gently upon on the morning of our own great judgement where we must account for the autonomous life that we lived?

The dark forces lurk in the spaces between life and death. When a baby is aborted from the womb of its mother and denied entry into life, it is the dark forces of death that once more reigns within our world. The medical profession can identify problems that may arise with the development of a life within its mother's womb and this it can be determined early so that a termination will result.

We are the sole arbiters of life and death within this world. We are always calculating, always plotting, always determining what is the best outcome for our lives but we always fail to recognise that the life we have been given is not ours to barter with. We don't own the life that we reside within. We never chose this life that we inherited but we are now here and living this precious but complex life. Everything that we do and everything that we say has a consequence and a reaction to this life and possibly for beyond.

The great enemy of the light that lives in us is the darkness that wishes to destroy us. The dark forces are never too far away from us. They are always showing us the open road along endless space that is of yet to be experienced. When we walk along that road and submit to the temptations of our lives, then the light that once shone so bright has now been dimmed as the dark forces clamour for our body and soul.

When Adolf Hitler set out to find and raise a strong Aryan culture of people, it was decided that any physical life that was impure and imperfect could not be allowed to survive and death was the inevitable outcome. The medical profession today can identify such defects and imperfections in the growing body and because the developing child is not developing in a natural state, then it is legally acceptable for that child to be terminated from life.

The combination of the medical and legal professions given law by governments and, in the end, chosen by the mother are all the dark forces that hinder the light within life. Each action we take in the darkness must eventually be accounted for within the light, as all those lives that were prevented from existing must all be accounted for too. No life that was ever created truly disappears from existence. The darkness desires for such life to dissolve into the emptiness, whereas the light must confront such darkness with the truth.

Life is not only hindered and taken at its inception but also in the closing stages of a life when a human being can decide to depart this world and thus will seek help to assist them to pass from this world. In the world, we call this assisted suicide because the person no longer wants to live in this world but legally require an assistance to take their own life.

There are many places throughout our world that welcome and assist the human being who no longer wants to live. They will help such a person but their motives are for financial gain and not out of some form of compassion where they want to be there by the dying person's bed before they pass. Assisted suicide is fraught with complications because at its centre is often a human being who may be gravely ill and in constant suffering whilst there are so many legal issues that first need to be addressed before granting such a wish.

There is a deep sadness to assisted suicide because once a decision has been made and granted then the course of action will follow to its unnatural conclusion when the life of the person will end in the quietness of a room and in the warmth of a bed. The doctors are yet again present as they administer the fatal dose into the body of the still human. As the fatal drugs enter the bloodstream of its recipient, the body begins to shut down and fade away from its once existence. The dark forces combine with the doctor who administers the fatal dose and the specific drugs that were planned for in advance in detail so as to ensure that the life will permanently stop within that human being. The singular and eroded life that developed so naturally in the internal world now succumbs to life in the external world surrounded by corruption and darkness.

At the heart of all human life is the connection between our full autonomy and our choice to self-destruct at any time in order to end our life. It is a tragedy that we are so flawed as a human species but to be allowed to physically take the life that we once had but do not own shows us that we were originally programmed to die. If a human being never left their home and joined society, we still have the potential to hurt, to suffer and ultimately die.

We can hide away for years in our rooms in order not to hurt others but at any moment we can pick up a number of weapons that are readily available to us and strike such a weapon into our body in order to stop the life living within. There is only one question a person can ask when rationally contemplating on such an outcome and that is simply why?

Why have human beings been trusted enough to be given full autonomy over our lives and even to the ultimate end of self-destruction? If there is an all-knowing and all-loving creator who gave us the gift of life then why would such a gift come with self-destruction as another form of taking a human life from existence? How many human lives since human beings first came onto the Earth have ended due to a self-destructing suicide?

To take one's life in this world is illegal and one of great taboo but how can the aggressive perpetrator and intended victim stand trial to an injustice committed onto the world when they are no longer alive to make such a defence for their own actions?

We live in such an unequal world and there are deep inequalities and injustices experienced by human beings. One human being could be born into wealth and experience a comfortable life, while later on in life that same person may be confronted with deep suffering where it questions their own existence and meaning in life. That person who was once happy and secure is now sad, alone and turns in on itself.

The suffering internal does not stop even when sleep comes. Their dreams become an extension of the daily suffering and at any time a decision can be made to depart this life by self-destruction. There is a great sadness to all our life and existence. This is the only life we know and how can we be certain that upon death that another life will begin for us?

We never asked to come into this world but still we are here to live by the rules and ways of life that have been set forth for us. The body that we have autonomy within instinctively wants to live but knows that one day our ultimate fate is to die. We can never escape such a reality. It follows us through all the moments of our lives, especially the moments that we are truly happy because at such a moment we are living the life that we were supposed to live. Death is patient and death is silent too. The ending must be an extinguishing of the light from the body of the human.

The self-destructing moment for any human being is one of great loneliness. The person could have decided that they wish to finally leave this world but will not depart due to some painful illness of the body. Instead, they wish to slowly exit on their own terms within their own body. Once the decision has been made, it remains permanent and a course of decisive action will follow. The person will begin to finalise their earthly affairs and try to undo any wrongs that they felt were committed by them along their journey. They will go and spend some time with their close friends and perhaps may give to others various possessions that they once owned on the earth but have not a need for any longer. The mind speeds up and it soon decides on the time, place and suitable weapon to assist in order to depart its life. Perhaps the family of the person will be the last people to see him or her before that moment arrives. The great flaw of our humanity is always there because we know that if life is not a place we desire to be in any longer, then the autonomy that was granted to us at birth will be there to allow us to walk on that final journey to the darkness. Our corrupted world aides in our self-destruction because there are many weapons to choose from that human beings once created. There is, of course, the assault rifle which on impact will destroy the physical body permanently. There is also a physical rope that can hang from a solid object and the person can be attracted to such a still object because it too requires a stillness to its life. The self-destructing person may decide to take chemicals as an overdose, which again, when entering the body, will cause an assault onto its organs as they slowly begin to fade and fight at the same time. The self-destructing person may decide to return to the water because we are born from the waters of life and into the waters our lives will finally cease to exist. Whatever manner of implementation is decided, the final moments are of great sadness because it is time to say goodbye to the life the person once knew. When the impact finally happens, the forces of good and the forces of bad that have always been with the person in life are still there as death comes knocking at their door. The person wants to go and has decided to do so but the physical body will still fight for the life within the occupier as it has always done so instinctively throughout the life of the person. The ending of all life is again a joining together of the good and the bad; of the light and of the darkness. The moment of impact is a surge to the physical body and a chaotic rupturing to its internal organs. There is no romantic ending to a life but the dark forces that are always within us have won yet another battle against our humanity.

Chapter 12
Philosophies of Life

Is there a genuine hope for our humanity or are we destined to make the same mistakes as our predecessors did due to the simple fact that we are human? Perhaps the optimist within us can look for hope as it is close to a century since the last world war and global states realise that the devastation to their culture, lands and people is too much compared to momentary victory and acquisition of land space.

If and when the time comes that humanity decides on a true course of action that will ultimately bring about global peace to our planet, then such solutions must come from within each human being in order to bring about a collective change. A whole new education and a desire for wisdom needs to take place within each person in order to eradicate pre-conceived and illogical beliefs that have been part of us and our identity since our own childhoods.

Each culture, country and people need to see how we allow the cancer of racism to continue its spread through our planet. When I was a boy, we used to play a game called cowboys and Indians. The cowboys were the good guys and they were white in colour. The Indians were the bad guys and they were dark in colour. We all wanted to be the cowboys as we wanted to chase around the Indians and to hurt them.

At such a young and impressionable age, I did not know anything about racism but I had inherited such racist undertones and a belief system that came to me through entertainment on the big and small screens. I used to watch many western movies with my father and we always applauded along for the good cowboys who chased around the bad Indians. Guns were always in the hands of both the cowboys and Indians as they rode their horses in desolate places, whereby the humans and horses became the centre of existence and the environment was the backdrop to such action.

When I look back at such moments from childhood, it makes me feel both sad and angry because I realise now how terrible racism is within humanity. It was later on at school when I learned about how human beings bought and sold other human beings as part of the slave trade. The wealthy white owner would buy the poorer person of colour and then chain and shackle their property in acts of horrendous racism and the abuse of innocent human beings.

History's slavery is comparable to the Holocaust because at the centre of such darkness was a warped belief system that one culture and people is above another culture and people and the dark forces will always go on the offensive to show their strength manifested as pure hatred with violence over the innocent and submissive victims of racism.

In my country of Ireland, we are racist but it is against people of the same colour, the Travelling Community. For generations, the Travelling Community have been treated appallingly by settled Irish people because they were seen as beneath Irish people and were trodden upon both physically and psychologically. Settled Irish people became the aggressors and the discriminators against the innocent Travelling Community. I remember at school hearing derogatory comments made by settled people against the Travelling Community. There were no Travelling Community children at any school that I attended and yet such divisive and racist comments became normal on our small island. The young children who made such comments in the school yard learned such words within their own homes and found it natural to reproduce them at school because there were no travelling children there to defend themselves but crucially not one of our teachers ever defended the Travelling Community either by admonishing the children making such comments. When I look back now at such times, I feel disgusted because these people of the Travelling Community are every bit as Irish as I am and yet they were knocked down and degraded for a traditional way of life that was at the very heart of the Travelling Community. Racism against the Travelling Community was not challenged and so no education took place or wisdom sought as ingrained racism and tribalism grouped together in aggression to label such innocent victims. I grew up within a council housing estate near the centre of Galway city and within the estate I lived in were many families from the Travelling Community. It always confused me as a child as I thought if a person was a Traveller, then they must be in a constant movement of travel on the road and yet these families were living in houses just as I was. My father taught me at a young age that these families are the very same as we are and that

103

I was never to say any degrading comments towards them. I was lucky that I had two parents who had a morality-based sense of justice and that they saw everybody as equal. I remember going on a journey once with my father when I was a teenager. We went to a funeral home where a person from the Travelling Community had passed away. My father wanted to go there to pay his respects to the deceased family members. When we arrived there, I remember how they all knew my father and were so thankful to him for attending the removal of one of their own people. It made me feel proud that I had a father who saw in them, a people who were exactly like everybody else and such outward behaviour of sincerity shown by my father educated me to behave in such a manner. That event took place a long time ago when I was a very young boy and yet my mind remembers and recalls it because it was a moment of education, of learning and of wisdom for me that I was never taught in all those years in the classroom. When it came time for my father to pass away, I recall how many people from the Travelling Community came to our home to pass on their sympathies over the loss of the patriarch of our family.

Moral behaviour that is given will be shown and it will return in equally a moral and a just manner. There is another minority group in Europe that have for generations, been subjected to deep forms of discrimination and racism. They are the Roma culture of Eastern and Southern Europe. I remember learning about the Roma culture through movies, television news reports and at school in history class. I never recall any positive reports about the Roma culture. Everything that was reported was negative, racist and vitriolic. This is a culture of people who, along with the Jews, were almost wiped out after they were deliberately sent to the gas chambers throughout Europe during the Holocaust to die for no other reason than having been seen as a lower form of humanity. Where was the empathy and sensitivity shown towards the surviving Roma people after 1945? Their culture and people continue to be discriminated against as it is easy for racist human beings to go on the offensive and to speak all kinds of calumny against such people because it fits in with their divisive world view and narrative. There is a caste system here in Europe just like there was for centuries in India. It is an unofficial caste but certainly the Roma culture of Europe throughout history were seen to be placed at the lowest level of humanity. I would often recall hearing how both Bulgaria and Romania are dirty places, because that is where the gypsy people reside. Such racist outbursts need to be challenged and when I visited both Bulgaria and Romania, they were not the places that such racists spoke about. In fact, they were the very opposite. I spent a lot of time in both Plovdiv of Bulgaria and Bucharest in Romania, where Roma culture dwells. I witnessed there a peaceful people with a long tradition dating back centuries within Europe. These are a people with a traditional way of life and it is wrong for others to treat them as some form of lower species. Their culture and life have a right to continue because they are human beings like any other human beings on this planet.

When we only stay within our own lands and learn about others, there is often an insular outlook that we form and maintain. We learn a narrative about other lands and peoples and such narrative becomes quickly fixed and set in place. Invariably, everything we learn about other places and peoples are not factual in reality. They are mostly stereotypes and snippets of stories that add to how we view others from where we reside. However, if and when we take the courage to visit such lands and peoples, the stereotypes that we carried with us for all those years will quickly dissipate and suddenly we are just left with the people who stare back at us.

We then begin to see who they really are and we realise that they are very similar to us because of our shared humanity. We need to begin to see in minority cultures such as the Travelling Community in Ireland and the Roma culture in Eastern and Southern Europe that their cultures and ways of life need to be respected, cherished and above all they need to be seen and respected as equals if we are going to find that elusive peace that we truly seek.

Along with racism, we also need to look within ourselves at how we all treat the marginalised, the vulnerable, the physically and mentally ill within our societies and globally. Instead of feeling pity for a person who is blind or deaf, we can instead show empathy and support to such people as valuable citizens within society. A person who cannot see externally can still use the other senses that they were born with but just require some extra support and patience from the rest of us who are lucky enough to have the gift of sight. When we show such empathy to others, it slowly breaks down any form of division or pre-conceived ideas about another person and then at a basic level without interference we can come together as simply one person meeting another person regardless of culture, sex, religion, politics or beliefs. We never fully see or understand what lives in the heart and mind of another. We could see a person in society who uses a wheelchair because they have lost their ability to stand and walk. The nature of such a sight is that we would usually show some form of humanity to that

105

person, but what if we encountered a person who we did not know has an underlying physical or mental illness? Doesn't that person deserve the same clemency that we showed towards the person in a wheelchair and the person who lost their sight? The morality of such moments is that we should aim for pathos towards every person we meet because the more sensibility we give, the less hate that will exude outward from us.

For centuries, women have been seen as not only the fairer sex but also the sex of submission and second to the dominant male. As humans, we do not choose our sex just like we do not choose human life in the very first place. A determinant of our gender is chosen within our mother's womb in a biological manner. We are given a gender of male or female at birth and this becomes part of our identity as we move from childhood to adolescence and into adulthood.

History has, at many different stages, shown how the dominant male has abused the submissive female. It is yet another example of the dark forces working within humans, whereby the aggressor will use its strength on an offensive path in order to dominate its female victims. A woman's duty and life is no longer acceptable to be placed solely in the family home, giving birth to and raising children. She is not an object for sexual pleasure and then a commodity to carry such life into the world.

All of us human beings have a mother, whether we know her or not. She is the person who helped create us and then we developed within her womb before she gave birth to us so that our human life on Earth could begin. Every male on this planet has life because he was created by both his parents and then lived within the womb of his mother upon entry into the world. There are still many places throughout our world where women are abused and used as sexual slaves for the voracious lust within the male. Women are still used as sexual commodities and trafficked throughout the world and it is always the dominant and abusive male who uses their strength, aggression and greed in order to accumulate voluminous amounts of wealth whilst destroying the humanity within the female. It is ironically within various religions that the female consistently is given the role beneath the male, which is yet another example of the abuse of the male over the female.

In religion, the male is often taught that God created the male first and that the female was then created from the male. Males use this concept to discriminate against the females and to place them in a secondary role to themselves. As human beings, with a collective wisdom and appreciation, we need to begin to understand that women are not sent to this Earth for the sexual pleasure of men. They are not destined to or fated to be sexual slaves, prostitutes or be part of games constantly at the demands of men.

Women in the 21st century must be seen as equal in all aspects of life to men. They have a right for equal pay, equal status and are no longer to be seen as secondary to males. Throughout history, the male of the species have been taught and learned to go on the offensive and lead by way of aggression in order to define their gender role not only as head of their family but as a collective within their society, tribe and nation. History has also proved to us that such action by the male ultimately fails and leads to the breakdown of not only relationships within the family but a breakdown of moral values as human beings. The male of the 21st century and beyond needs to be different and needs to behave differently. The strength of the male no longer needs to be quantified by their physical prowess. They do not need to lead or be led by their sexual drive. The new male can be a leader within his own family, community and nation by being a caring and virtuous man in learning the true morality and wisdom come from our hearts and brains and not with violence through our bodies.

If we are to unite fully as a species, then we need to accept how we have treated other lifeforms on this planet within the natural world and the animals we share this world with. Our history and relationship with both have been fraught with abuse, cruelty, neglect and an apathy towards other life that is seen as beneath our own.

When I went to India a few years ago, I came into contact with the cow and saw there how it is revered and seen as sacred to all life. The cow is not a commodity for the pleasure and consumption of human beings. In India, the cow is a sacred being and is given full freedom and autonomy to live its life here on Earth. I remember when I first set foot onto the streets of Varanasi and at that particular moment I was confronted with seven bulls who were making their way down a street in my direction. I was naturally scared because my instinct informed me that these bulls could hurt me. Instead, the seven bulls walked past me but in doing so, stayed momentarily for me to greet them by touching their soft bodies. It was a moment of instant pleasure and happiness for me. I was so excited to be that close to a bull and yet there was no danger. It was a meeting between two species whereby each species is equal to the other and so both can interact and live alongside each other without any fear. On other occasions in India, I remember going on a train ride from New Delhi to Amritsar in the

Punjab. I had fallen asleep and I was awoken by gentle nibbling onto my right ear. I looked around and two soulful eyes stared back into my eyes. It was a delightful cow and immediately after nibbling on my ear, he strolled to a nearby door and another passenger opened the door for the cow to exit our carriage and move on into the next carriage. It was such an exquisite and surprising moment for me to witness. Later, at various temples, following prayer, I would receive some nuts from a Hindu holy man and was told that often they are given to the cows who sit nearby at the entrance to the temples. The feeding of nuts to a placid and fully living cow as its long tongue opens and accepts my offering is such a rare moment of love within our broken world.

I first became a vegetarian as a teenager after having watched a documentary on the full life of a pig from their birth to their death at the slaughterhouse. I had nightmares for weeks following that documentary and I could not sleep but think about the injustice that took place for those innocent pigs. A light went on in my brain with both anger and compassion in equal measure and from that moment onward I decided that as long as I would live on this Earth that I would never again consume an animal.

Animals throughout the world are only seen as commodities and a means to gain wealth when their gentle bodies are slaughtered for their meat. Farmers will buy and sell cows, pigs, sheep, goats and raise such life on their lands by placing them into large packs and feeding them so that they will increase in size and then at some stage early in the animals life it will no longer be deemed useful and then the innocent animals will be sent to a slaughterhouse. The final stage of the process happens in secret, away from humanity. The once living animals are stunned by an electric current that knocks the life out of them as their heart stops beating and their brain collapses and turns off. The animal is then cut up and hung before it is taken down and packed away into containers for its final delivery to butchers and supermarket chains. The last stage is when the human being will purchase the once living animal but who is now simply cold and dead meat in a package. The once living animals will fade away when the human being will eat its cooked body and digest into nothingness. The once living animals will then be defecated by the human as waste into the sewers. Then the process begins all over again and it is never-ending.

We treat marine life in the same manner. They live within their natural habitat but the aggressive human will invade their homes with a man-made device cunningly planned and set into the waters. The human lures the living fish with a bait and as the fish bites onto the bait it is attacked by a sharp blade that hooks onto the fated fish. The human then unwinds the rod and up comes the fish as it scrambles for survival out of its own environment. The fish then drops to the floor of the boat or the earth beside the human. It then wriggles around as it is gasping for oxygen. Its life ends moments later and then the human becomes its own butcher as it cuts up the meat and places the once living fish into a box before going home and cooking such meat before it is consumed into nothingness.

Human beings will strategically plan on which animals will be used for their meat and which animals will be used for human pleasure and wealth. For many cultures throughout the world, the dog is seen as man's best and closest friend but in some countries, the dog is used as a commodity for their meat. I went to Vietnam a few years ago and one evening when I was out walking the streets of Hanoi I came upon a restaurant and outside I witnessed one of the saddest sights in the history of my life. There was a wooden pen there and inside the pen was a poised but confused dog. This dog was on the menu to be consumed as food by the guests in the restaurant. It was so shocking to see this living life but knowing that soon this living and breathing dog would be killed in a manner that I cannot think about and then cut up before being placed into the kitchen for the chef to cook the dog's meat. This is human behaviour. This is what we are capable of and this is what we plan and set out to do. The dark forces are never too far away from us. We constantly look for new ways to reveal our true identities and when the dark forces have been fulfilled, we set out along our journey through the darkness once more because the taste of blood is so satisfying for the gluttony of man. In Ireland and in other countries, we couldn't imagine consuming a dog but the argument the Vietnamese might give to us would be, then why do we consume other animals like cows, pigs and sheep?

I have a cat at home. His name is Rizhik, which is Russian for ginger. He is a short-haired and domestic ginger cat and I love him very much. Rizhik's journey to our home was fraught with danger and almost did not happen. When Rizhik was born, it was decided by his owner that he was to be placed in a plastic bag and then thrown into the River Corrib in my city of Galway. My wife at that time learned of this cruel intention and she pleaded with me to take him to our home to both save his life and raise him as our own. I immediately said yes and so on a cold and dark Christmas Eve Rizhik as a tiny and two week old kitten entered our home, looked out from his cat box and made the first tentative steps into his new home and our lives. I sometimes think back to that episode when I look at Rizhik and it saddens me because he never knew how close he came to meeting a cruel death at the hands of the aggressive human. How often in life animals of all kinds are cruelly cast aside by the demands of the humans who take control and dominance over them.

Horses are another animal that have been used throughout human history. These stately, gentle and very sensitive creatures have had a history witnessing bloody battles forged over by empire against another empire as they carried the brutal humans with their many weapons of destruction. How many horses were murdered in such battles throughout history? Human history recounts the blood shed of humans against other humans but it never recounts how the innocent horses were used for such evil acts. Today all over our world horses are still used by human beings. They are bred by other horses and it is decided which horse has the best potential to win races carrying jockeys across various distances and assault courses, all in the name of wealth and prestige. Those horses who often fall during such dangerous races against other horses are the victims of serious injury and then the aggressive humans will decide to end the life of the horse by shooting it dead. The horse who is injured is of no use to the industry and so it is cast aside. Its name is rarely spoken of again and it disappears into obscurity.

How many diverse and innocent animals throughout our world are poached, hunted and murdered by humans just so that we can profit from various parts of their bodies? The ivory tusks of elephants and the horns of rhinoceros are hunted because such commodities create extensive wealth throughout the black market of illegal animal trafficking. The hands of gorillas are a prize throughout the world and is used as an ashtray by the incredibly stupid and insensitive human beings. How many human beings go out with their guns and shoot living birds dead just for the pleasure of the hunt? Is it an innate jealousy on the part of human beings that such delicate creatures have the ability to fly gracefully in the air, which is a feat that we can never accomplish? Why would we be allowed the freedom to fly when we have created so much devastation while on land? How many exotic birds are captured throughout the world and then placed in cages so that humans will buy them and then place them in another cage? The natural instinct of any bird is to fly in the air and not to be captured in a small cage. This abuse by human beings onto innocent animals will continue because as long as human beings demand meat from an animal or are willing to wear clothing, jewellery created from an animal's body, then the hunt for such animals will not stop. This aggression and dominance shown by humans onto animals is indicative of the dark forces raging within our soul. Only we can choose to stop it.

There are two certainties that I hold up as truths to live by in this life. The first is that I was born and have a life. The second certainty I hold true is that one day I will cease to exist and die from this life. The former is a historical fact that I have no recollection of but the latter will be an event that I will witness on a very personal level. The great equaliser to all human lives is that each and every human being that ever lived on this planet will at some point begin to break down and either in an instant or through a long process, the once human life will die and cease to exist.

Human illness is as natural for the human being as is our human health but as empathetic human beings we do not like to see other people suffer. The first time I ever saw somebody cry in my life was when my grandmother died and I saw tears roll down the cheeks of my father. I was only a little boy then and I could not grasp the magnitude of the situation, but when I witnessed my father crying, I felt what I now understand to be empathy as all I wanted to do was to go over and hug my father. Five years later, my second grandmother died and I then witnessed my mother crying, which was only the second time in my life to witness another person shedding tears. Ever since those early days of my childhood, I equate tears and crying with dying and death. I did experience people crying on television through movies but it never felt real for me and so I did not grasp the connection between a person crying and the loss of a person close to them whereas when I witnessed my parents crying I was moved to cry myself. I never got to experience the death of my grandfather's as they had succumbed to death before my entrance to life here on Earth.

The death and passing of one's mother has got to be one of life's most saddest events because when we ponder on the loss of a mother such memories will take us all the way back to within our mother's womb before she gave birth to us to enter life. When she passes, it is as though the physical location of our historical past and identity has been erased and that place of warmth and security has finally departed this Earth, never to return again. When the matriarch of any family dies, a crack appears to the rest of the family and such a crack can never again be healed or repaired. When the second parent dies, the loss is permanent as the children of those dead parents are now orphans. The loss of one's parents informs the children that there is an inevitability about all our lives whilst at the same time we recognise that the natural process and order to all life dictates if allowed to be that the parents must pass first before their offspring. When we are young, we live through the erratic and developing within our own minds. Nothing is really ever explained to us and so we never have a full understanding of what we are witnessing.

My mother's mother died when I was just ten years old. She had been ill for many years and I never got to see her stand up and walk. She was always sitting in a comfortable chair beside the open fire when I would visit her at different times each year. I asked my parents many times why granny Reilly was not walking and they always replied that she had severe arthritis and so this prevented her from standing up and moving. Human illness is always there waiting for its grand moment to arrive in order to surprise the witnesses and to also create a change and a suffering from the life they once knew. My uncle Pat or Pak as we affectionately called him, died in 1998 from a long and sufferable illness called multiple sclerosis. When I was a young boy, uncle Pak was a giant to me. He could pick me up and hold me in just one hand and the physical size of his body matched the size, the depth and the gentleness of his personality. We often refer to such people as gentle giants but uncle Pak was one such gentle giant. I never remembered the exact moment I heard that uncle Pak was ill because the medical term multiple sclerosis did not have any connection or understanding for my young mind. I just recalled seeing my uncle sitting in that same comfortable chair beside the fire that my grandmother had sat in a decade before. The parallels between my grandmother and my uncle were significant because never again did I witness my uncle Pak stand up and walk around. A debilitating illness had entered his body and attacked him so severely that it had knocked the once physically strong man that he was into a silent, broken and frail human being.

I always remember my mother as a physically strong woman both in body and in mind and to this day at 82 years of age she is still going strong even though she has severe arthritis passed on from the gene of her own mother. Her own mother lost her ability to walk in her 50s and yet my mother is still standing in her 80s if not upright at least standing in a curved manner as though she is raging against the illness that once took the life of her own mother and is now within her body too. The key to my mother's health is although her physical body is declining due to the ravages of time and age her mind is still very lucid and fully functioning and the messages her mind sends to the body and its organs is to continue working and fighting for the life within her.

I remember my father as having many illnesses throughout his life. Before I was born, he lost the middle finger on his left hand to an accident with a machine in the workplace. I was fascinated as a child because he would play games with me by pretending that he had lost a finger even though it was not pretending, as there was a vacant space between his fingers where the decapitated finger once resided.

When I was two years old, my father broke a disc in his back from an accident again at the workplace and for a long time after my memories of him were that of lying in a bed of a hospital. My father did recover but the various illnesses continued to find his body. My father had very poor eyesight and used to wear very large and thick-rimmed glasses in order to navigate his everyday world. A few years before he died, my father contracted prostate cancer and was given two choices. He could go on a course of chemotherapy by trying to attack the cancerous tumour with radiation or he could choose to undergo surgery to remove the same cancerous tumour. He chose the latter as he wanted the physical cancer to be removed in its entirety. Following the surgery, my father asked for his once prostate gland with its cancerous tumour attached to return home with him in a protective dish. I could not understand such a request but a few days later I was called into the sitting room and there on the table was one of the most revolting things I had ever seen. There in the silver dish lay the remains of my father's prostate gland and enveloping the gland was the cancerous tumour, which by then had turned a putrid purple in colour. What my father said next to me has remained in my collective consciousness ever since. He looked up at me and then looked down towards his prostate gland and said, 'I beat it.' I then understood why such an odd request had been made to his surgeon. We never really know what processes are taking place deep within our bodies but when my father got to stare straight into the cancerous tumour that ravaged his prostate gland he was indeed correct in stating that although his prostate gland was sacrificed, he still had life and health within his body. Shortly after his victory over cancer, another more aggressive illness attacked his body from the inside. He was diagnosed with chronic emphysema due to a narrowing of his lungs because of a lifetime of smoking cigarettes and an addiction to nicotine. The great irony was that he had given up smoking five years previously and the addiction had long since been defeated. Sadly, he was told by his doctor that it takes about five years for the physical remnants of smoking to leave a smoker's body if there is no lasting damage and the key word if became the central word for my father because there was significant physical damage to the lining and walls of his lungs. Chronic emphysema was an illness that I witnessed so closely because, as each day passed, I saw a deterioration to the health of my father. The nebuliser was given in order to help him control the airways to his lungs but the nebuliser is only an artificial machine and it can never replicate the benevolence of the working lungs as throughout our lives these two lungs continue to fight for the life within us and allow us to breathe in and out as normally and as effortlessly as we do until an illness sets in. The years of smoking cigarettes had left tar surrounding the once workable lungs and such damage was irreversible. One evening I returned home from work and as I entered our sitting room, I saw my father laying on the floor with his hand outstretched trying to grasp at the nebuliser as he had fallen whilst gasping for the oxygen that his body desperately needed. It was so sad for me to witness a man that was always so strong, so caring and so honourable to be reduced to such helplessness as his body began to break down from within.

I wish that I could report the final few days and hours of my father's life as gentle and quiet ones but such an illness does not allow for romantic idealism. My father was rushed to the hospital on St Patrick's Day and left his home for the final time. For the next three days, it was a slow and agonising process of the dying of a body from the dark forces of illness that had entered his body. When I visited him in that hospital bed, I saw a metamorphosis of the man I once knew. His face had stretched outward like a balloon full of air. The air in that face was the artificial air from the nebuliser as it tried in vain to allow him to breathe. The tarred lungs had narrowed and the air could not enter nor depart in its natural state. My father's voice also changed into a high pitch tone as the life of this human being tried to hold on for as long as he possibly could. I wasn't there for the final moments of my father's life as my mother had asked me to go and contact our priest to come and bless his dying body. The abiding memory I hold of those final hours sitting in silence and helplessly looking at my gravely ill father was how I witnessed the physical manifestation of the dark force internally coming out externally onto his face. I knew he was fading but I longed for a miracle from the light to defeat such darkness within the walls of that room. I could not stop staring into my father's eyes. There was a sadness, a longing and a fear within those small eyes as the illness was circling in and around them.

Everything had aged in my father but the eyes within him did not age. The eyes within all of us remain constant even when the rest of our body begins to crumble. The darkness within fought the light aggressively and violently until the light could fight no more. The light then faded away as the darkness remained in its evil and egotistical state. I returned later to the hospital and when I entered my father's room I saw my mother sitting beside the empty space where my father last lay but he was gone now. The doctor entered soon after and all he said was "he is gone; he is dead".

The emotionless words from the doctor whose vocation it is to save lives indicated to me that often there is such an elitist and status inducing nature to the medical profession. We often hang all our hope on them but in the end death will always win in the fight against life. The success rate of all doctors is one of the lowest in all professions for the simple fact that every patient of a doctor throughout its entire career will die and furthermore the once great doctor will die too. I respect and admire doctors but it is the discerning and perceptive doctors like that of Anton Chekhov who I admire the most. He was a doctor but he was also a writer and so the sensitive, caring and creative sides of him fused with the scientific mind and there was a balance within him so that each patient he treated witnessed a profound mercy transferring from the doctor onto and into the patient. There is such a divisive element to the medical profession in the 21st century because so much of it is based around private medical insurance whereby wealth, status and legality come first before the true meaning of the Hippocratic Oath. Doctors and nurses are lost within a myriad of politics and legality. They want to help the patient but often they are powerless to the inevitable dark forces that also lurk deep within the long wards of a hospital.

My father was just 63 years old when he died and if he had never smoked cigarettes, it was possible that he could still be living today. I was later informed by my father's doctor that my father had a physically working heart like that of a 35-year-old man which deeply saddened me because I began to think about how hard the heart must have worked in order to fight for his life but the erroneous lungs were beyond repair and so the heart did eventually stop beating to relinquish the life within. My father left behind a grieving widow along with a daughter and son who still miss him very much and try to live each day with the many lessons that he gave to us during his life. The people whom we have loved and lost in this life will never be forgotten. They will remain alive in our memories and in our good deeds. My father's name was Thomas.

One of the most criminal acts in this world is how tobacco companies are continuously allowed to legally sell their evil and body altering products. There is nothing of value in tobacco. It is a product that, when entering the human body through its oesophagus, distributes thousands of chemicals that attack the internal mechanisms of our physical form. The human being becomes addicted to nicotine at a young age and this is the winning formula for tobacco companies because an addicted smoker means continued profits and wealth for these evil empires on Earth. The tobacco companies are a physical manifestation of the dark forces making their way internally to the external world and it is there that they are allowed to continue unabated with their vile acts of killing human beings slowly.

Here in Ireland, our government collectively, instead of fighting such empires, allow them to continue their destructive forces within the bodies of mankind. Each year during our government's budget they will increase the cost of a packet of cigarettes but this is such an insult to humanity because the addictive smoker will still purchase the tobacco regardless of its cost. The only way to challenge such empires is to ban universally their death causing chemicals because it is now known for certain beyond any doubt that smoking cigarettes leads to illness and eventual death for its users.

Illness will always reside within the bodies of human beings due to the flawed nature of our lives. We live in a broken world and we are therefore a broken and suffering species. We can try so much throughout our lives to look after both our physical and our mental states but illness will find a way to enter our bodies. We could be lucky to avoid illness throughout our lives but the dark forces will eventually come for us and death will follow soon after.

When I was nineteen years old, I was diagnosed with an eye illness called macular degeneration. It did not mean anything to me then but as time went on and my headaches intensified and morphed into crippling and debilitating migraines especially within the quiet and dark hours in bed, I realised how such an illness attacks and how one day I might go blind as my retina becomes compromised and may stop the light from allowing me the gift of sight in this world.

It is a terrible and lonely existence to be fully conscious at night, staring at the walls and ceiling as they closed in on me due to the magnitude of the pain that was present at both ends of my temple. There is no place to hide at such moments. All I could do was to attach ice cubes to a headband in order for the

116

cold to fight against the severe heat that existed within my head. The nights were long as I cried myself in and out of sleep due to the pressure and pain that existed in combination with each other. Even when the sun would rise the next morning, the pain would not have subsided and followed me around until I could fight the pain no more and just wallowed in the acceptance of such trauma to my body. I travelled extensively for many years because I thought my time for witnessing splendid images was coming to an end. I went to see so many places and had many experiences and always my scarred eyes saw and recorded such moments of the poetic for me. There is no price in this world or any other that one could pay for the gift of their healthy eyes. In the last few years, my eye doctor informed me that the scars that once lay next to my retina no longer reside there and those once shattering and debilitating headaches have now gone too. Is it possible that this once degenerative eye illness could have reversed itself within me so that now my eyes are healthy and alive? I know that one day my eyes will stop functioning and begin to break down and die just like the rest of my body will but that day is not today and I hope it will not be tomorrow either.

I remember learning about the horrendous and callous illness of Parkinson's disease that attacked the once boxer named Muhammad Ali. He was a man with a physically strong and healthy body and with an infectious personality that charmed so many people throughout this world. When Parkinson's disease entered his body, it completely altered the physical state of this once strong man.

I feel as angry about boxing as I do about cigarette smoking. Boxing just like cigarette smoking brings no value to human life. Boxing is a legal framework whereby violence is allowed to take place between human beings. Each boxer within the ring has an aim to knock down and out its opponent and it does so by striking that opponent into its body, face and, most shockingly, to the opponent's brain. Our brains are soft and delicate tissue, only protected by our skulls along its outer core. A continuous striking action to this fatigued and life allowing organ will overtime break down and destroy such tissue. Why are we so blind that we cannot see and understand that this form of legalised violence is a constant threat to our physical health and ultimately to our lives?

A similar dark force resides within the boxing world, just like it does within the tobacco companies. Boxing and its promotion earn large sums of wealth and profits for all who have a vestige interest in it but it is the brave boxers themselves who risk their lives each time they set foot into the ring. Each boxer is also responsible for the life of its opponent but they are blind to such reality.

If one boxer knocks another boxer down and that falling boxer dies within the ring, then is all worth it to see such violence and death all masked as entertaining sport?

I have a friend named Malachy. He is one of my oldest and dearest friends. I have known him since I was twelve years old and I trust him as I trust my own heart. Malachy suffers from the illness autism. When I met him in the first year at secondary school, I didn't know anything about autism and nor did I care. Malachy was just my friend and the person with whom I would meet up with each weekend during the year to go along to the movies with. I didn't have to learn about this illness in a book or through the medical profession. Malachy slowly revealed this illness to me that plagued both his body and mind. I never knew Malachy before his autism so he was always simply my friend without having labels attached to him. Malachy is a human being who just so happens to suffer with autism in a similar way that I am a human being who just so happens to suffer with macular degeneration. Sometimes in life, a person's illness will reveal a hidden meaning to all our lives and Malachy's illness has revealed to me how I can be a more empathetic and loving person towards others without judging them on the external physical body that is shown to me. Our humanity and light that always resides within us can shine outward and still live a life worthy of our own humanity.

Every illness known to man or every illness that will be known to man in the future is an inevitable dark force within our flawed humanity whose aim it is to eradicate our physical and mental bodies until those languid bodies will break down and succumb to the driving force of death as it knocks on the walls of our beating hearts.

The human body in which we reside is the only permanent home that we have ever known and so we must fight within this corrupted body of ours from birth until our death arrives. How lucky we are to be alive at all and to have reason within us. We instinctively know that we are going to die and yet what a gallant battle that can be, as the light in us stands firm and faces the darkness for a battle we cannot win but still the light wants to live.

So, if you exist and are out there somewhere amidst this grand and mysterious space, then what is the meaning of our existence in a world where both the light and the dark are consistently opposing forces? After our human species have been here for thousands of years, have we really altered this planet in ways that are positive for our survival?

Death will come to all living things on this planet. Human, animal and plant life will all cease to exist one day. It is a mathematical certainty that death will come to the human body. From the moment we are born from our mother's womb and enter this world as living and breathing beings, we are on a slow journey towards death. The clock is ticking from the moment we took our first breath until we draw our last one to succumb to the inevitable destruction of life. It is our destiny for whatever reason that may be to die in this life. We are all born with the knowledge and burden that we will all die and cease to exist one day. The assault of death on the human body is irreversible and cannot be defeated. We can choose to ignore death and live our lives in both blindness and ignorance to what is staring us all in the face. We can choose to escape the challenge of death and fight it head on with the intention of becoming immortal. This would be an action of stupidity and would for certain end in failure and death for the individual. We can also try and slow the ageing process down by a means of artificial chemicals and cosmetic surgeries to search for the fountain of youth in order to try and cheat death. This again would end in failure as the body and its internal mechanisms of our DNA structure is programmed and are slowly decomposing from birth until its fading and elimination at death.

What is the solution for the corruption and dark forces that are present within our species? Is it really possible that our human species at some point in the future could find that elusive acceptance of one another and live together in peace? It has not been witnessed since the arrival of human beings so is there any reason to believe that we could change?

We have so much desire within to climb forth from this planet of ours and to discover new planets in the universe but if we were to travel beyond our own world then surely we would take with us this corruption that has been alive within us since our birth and infect other planets and species with our own inherent evil.

We always hold onto the belief that we are special and set apart in the universe but what if at some point in the future that other intelligent life will be found and perhaps such intelligent life will find us before we locate them? Perhaps other intelligent life within the universe have been observing us but has decided not to come our way because we are much too precarious a species and how can we unite with another life when we have tried continuously to destroy our own species and home?

That takes us back again to we the guardians of this small and round planet suspended within a never-ending space in the universe. What can we do to solve the puzzle of our existence?

Nothing we have done in the past millennia has brought about a peace in our world so logically we need to find new ideas, philosophies and systems so that they can benefit all living life on Earth and not just a select few. There is an urgent need to look at our political structures through the continents of the world and within such structures it is the use of nation states and nationalism that have continued to divide us more than unite us as a species.

Each citizen of the world is locked into a political structure of some kind and they belong to a nation state. A nation state does provide autonomy and security for its citizens but when we belong to one nation state, that particular state becomes most important and the other nation states fade into our collective amnesia and apathy. I am a citizen of one nation state named Ireland within a larger family of collective nation states known as the European Union. This means that first and foremost my loyalties and thoughts are to my country and then towards my continental family but how do such nationalistic loyalties and tribalism lead to a cohesion of peoples throughout the planet?

The history of nationalism has shown us how the dark forces within our species have been unleashed by the stronger and more strategically planned nations as they begin to inflict an aggression in the form of an invasion to the smaller and less aggressive nations. The danger is always with such larger nations as their collective memory recalls past glories for their once mighty empires. Such larger nations could see a leader elected that does not have any sense of morality for his people and land. When such a moment arises, the nation state becomes inherently nationalistic and they begin to look outward at other smaller nations in order to invade, destroy and conquer. When we are nationalistic, we think inwardly of our own nation and people and when that is satisfied we begin to look externally towards other nations but such external thoughts are not moralistic in virtue and so a danger of the dark corruptive forces within could be unleashed externally once more. We all take pride in where we are from. We love our country and rightfully so but our national identity is only formed accidently by our birth and so any nation in the world could have potentially been our home. We all belong to some home and we have our own particular flag, national colours, national anthem and often a national language and this brings us immense collective security but in the end such an idealism is limited and deeply divisive to ourselves as a species. We need to change how we see our true identity on this planet. At this point in time, we have not found any other higher ordered species away from our planet so there is a sense that we are alone. However, if this changes and one day we get a visit or an aggressive invasion by another intelligent life like ourselves, then how we see one another within nation states becomes redundant and obsolete. On that day, it won't matter what country and culture we are from. It will only matter that we are one human species united in our own home. There is a need and urgency for us to become united as a species here on Earth. How we achieve this will be deeply complex due to the many divisions within each culture and our pre-conceived judgements and fears of other peoples. Isn't it strange that we have multiple national anthems and flags on this planet but why don't we have a universal anthem and flag that unites and not as individual states but as a collective and united human species? Nationalism does not and will never work for one very simple fact and that is, our world is inherently evil, divided and unequal and as long as these three stumbling blocks remain intact, then nationalism and our nation state structure is doomed for continuous failure. How can one poorer nation state be seen as equal to a wealthy nation state when that wealthy nation state has its own collective and inward goals that do not concern the poorer state? This is inequality and a whole new set of structures need to be applied so that equality for all cultures and peoples are a basic human right and not some form of idealistic hope that may never become a reality for its marginalised people. A universally based structure of politics and governance can work if there is unity amongst all peoples of the world upon entering such a structure. Our current system of national governments does not work because in times of conflict, one stronger nation who attacks a weaker nation and takes that weaker nations resources for their own will not be challenged in any universal manner to stop such forms of aggression. At this time in the early 21st century, there has been ongoing civil war in Syria where many of its people have been killed in a prolonged campaign of bombings and yet most nations in the world are powerless to intervene in order to assist Syria and their people. We are powerless because we fall under nationalistic governments and consequently, if a conflict and war is happening far away, then it does not concern us. However, if such a conflict was to appear on our own lands through an invasion, then it would concern us and as a result we would react accordingly. Nation states cannot come to the aid of other nation states and therein lies the inequality of our political systems and governance. As individual nation states, we are all powerless to stop the collective drive to spread drugs and arms throughout our planet. A plant can grow naturally in one land and then through a collective scale of manufacturing and transport that once growing plant can be used by people illegally all over the world where the lure of profits and wealth drives the dark forces within such cartels. The individual drug user can over time become addicted to such drugs and a spiralling journey continues for the slaves to such drugs. A world structure in governance would allow an attack on such dark forces whereby one system of equality will work together in order to stamp out the spread of such a stain on our humanity. The very same ideology could be used to stamp out the evil arms trade. How many human beings are aware that factories dotted throughout our planet exist in order for weapons to be manufactured and then those same weapons will be transported and shipped to designated places but especially to areas of conflict and war? The arms manufacturers and dealers are mostly nation states where conflicts are not ongoing but such nation states will be driven by the greed of wealth and an immoral apathy towards such zones of conflict. The lands who are at war nationally or civilly are in danger, where a threat to their culture and people is very real. They will purchase such weapons so that they can be placed in the hands of their own citizens in order to continue the cycle of conflict. After thousands of years of human conflict, can we now see that war between nations and peoples is an absurdity? Nothing good and of value comes from conflict and war. Even if we win a war by defeating and killing a people, the blood that was spilled throughout the battlefields of those same people will be taken up and replaced by their inheritors who will then fight until their deaths in order for justice to be carried out for their loved ones and citizens. These inheritors will then chase us eternally until our blood is spilled in revenge for their people. We cannot go and invade the homes and lands of another culture and people, pillage their resources and try to cleanse them from existence without a response from the invaded. Even when we do successfully invade a country and win a war, we ultimately lose our soul and the morality that we inherited from our birth. All wars, no matter how small or how legitimate in nature are ill-conceived, deranged and cannot be won. Nationalism and its ingrained ideology are at the centre of such conflict between nations. A universal style governance whereby nationalism is replaced by a collective system which is equal for all peoples and cultures will be one such way to try and challenge the evil forces of conflict and war. When nationalism is seen as the antithesis of humanity, then finally we can find a structure that is equal for all to work towards.

Language has divided us as a species since we first arrived onto the Earth. Multiple languages and cultures are something unique and of value to us as a people as language connects us to our culture and national identity. However, if we speak one language, how can we possibly connect with the many other languages and cultures? Language divides us more than it unites us. If two people across various continents meet up in a different land, how will they communicate with each other? Each will converse in their own native language but how will the other understand and how will acceptance and progress be made? The solution will be a universal style governance whereby our unique cultures will still be cherished as a link to our identity but we will still look to our future and a universal language common for all peoples throughout our world.

Monarchy and its aristocratic systems are the collective face of inequality from our past that still resides within our world today. The aristocratic way is not one of acceptance and equality for all people. Their way is a division between wealth and a lifestyle of luxury and greed compared with many people who live along the margins of society and cannot make any progress from their position because the system is naturally unequal.

Plato was correct using the teachings of Socrates when he called for the leaders of our political systems to become philosophers with a sense of a philosophical idealism and a moralistic virtue will become such a natural leader of people. There are many leaders of nations who do not hold such moral or philosophical ideals. They often govern or mostly dictate to their subjects through a system that is deeply flawed, divided and unequal for such citizens.

How can a nation lead its people if such a nation is ruled by a corrupted human being whose only desire is to ravage its people in order for such people to become submissive and slaves to their nation and leader?

A universal style structure of governance could exist and it could flourish if philosophical and morally virtuous people will take up such roles and lead their peoples. A universal style governance will be equal for all. It does not have any divisions or judgements about a person's culture, creed, sexuality. The goals of such an idealistic universal governance will put people at the centre of one's thinking and application. The vulnerable and, once marginalised, will find a voice because there will be no hierarchy or caste structure. Each individual becomes the moral collective. The pawn on the chessboard becomes the most important piece because the pawn instinctively knows that on either side of him is another pawn that is equal to him and assists his progress through life. There will no longer be a need for kings and queens and castles just like on a chessboard. Their former positions of privilege will be a memory from the past that can no longer be accepted because they never brought to the world an equality that we most desired.

The world we live in today is deeply divided, unequal and has no moralistic virtue. As a collective species, we have brought about a rampant chaos that has destroyed the concept and ingrained idealism that was once part of the light of humanity but now we linger mostly in the darkness because we can no longer see our way to the light. There is a plague that has always existed within our small planet and it has been moved by this driving force of darkness whose aim it is to destroy our world and remove the light and goodness that resides in us too. Within each person who lives is both the light and the dark. We have a choice which one of the forces we can live by. There is, of course, an inevitability of our death from this life and so as a result, the dark force will win at the end of our natural life when the light goes out from our humanity as the body fades and submits to death. However, as long as we continue to live in this natural life, we do have a choice between following the light and submitting to the dark. If we follow the light, then we have a moral obligation to live our lives as a testimony to such a light. If we choose a life amid the darkness, then we submit to that life and will live within the shadows of humanity. There will always exist a conflict within our bodies. We cannot avoid such conflicts because our natural human state was born to such conflicts. The only way we can avoid such conflicts is through an act of self-destruction or a natural death itself. We cannot reside in the body of any other human being throughout our life cycle so we have a choice to accept the conflict or to reject it. Either way, death will be the natural end to our earthly life and to our physical body. We can live our entire lives blind to the fact of our ultimate fate. The dark forces within urge us to live our life in the darkness and to cause chaos onto humanity because its rationale is that we are going to die in the end so why not always live in the darkness so that we can become accustomed to its destructive force?

As a collective human species, we are afraid of death and that is why we try to avoid it throughout our lives. The animal instincts within the human are selfish and try to ignore its impending death out of a complete fear of what death means and the possibility of a life beyond death strikes more fear into the animal instincts of the human. Everything will die upon our death. All of our ideals, all of our earthly possessions, all of our wealth, our memories, our cultures, everything must pass from this world. They are just the objective symbols from our earthly lives and the desires that we had while we lived but all of those objects must die too. The objective must never come before the subjective. The subjective is who we really are as a species and the love that dwells within us. This love must be relinquished too on death as everything is destined to pass and die. Perhaps then it is the final moments of our lives that become the most important as we lay dying and begin to contemplate on our existence and the true meaning for our lives. Whilst we are dying from this life, we could finally seek that moment of truth as we are faced with impending death. It could be that very moment in which we ask oneself: was my life truly lived and does my life hold any meaning for me now that I am dying?

As the sun was setting over the waters of Baikal, it was time for me to depart and make my way back to Irkutsk. Our lives are simply a finite number of days, coupled with a collection of experiences that we witness and carry with us as memories until it is our time to breathe our last and depart this world.

I am so happy that these scarred eyes got to witness the divine and inspired beauty of Lake Baikal. If one day these eyes will no longer see, then the meaning of this day will roll like a beacon of light into my soul. When I am an old man, I will look back upon my life and I will recall special days like this one. I was physically alone but yet she was here with me as she always seems to be lingering within the shadows of my soul.

Chapter 13
A Sunday Stroll

My final day in Irkutsk began along the Angara as I crossed the wooden bridge and made my way to the eternal flame and memorial to all those soldiers who lost their lives defending the Soviet Union during the Great Patriotic War. I am back in the busy and everyday life of the world once more but I long to be back in Listyvanka strolling along the promenade of Lake Baikal.

It is the natural world that excites me the most as it stirs up in me a feeling of stoicism and an acceptance of my place in the world. The flame burns continuously through a star and under a thick slab of concrete surrounded by the numerous fir trees on all sides. I sat on a bench and watched the many come and pay their respects beside the flame by laying flowers to honour their fallen dead. In close proximity to the eternal flame stands a large concrete building with the names of the dead soldiers etched onto its walls as a testimony to the nation that such honour and bravery will never be forgotten.

As I watched the children, I began to ponder on whether one day they too will be asked to serve mother Russia in the many battles that come their way. How can children so young truly understand the significance of such memorials? Their instincts are to play and enjoy their childhoods and not to be consumed by the affairs of the divided adults.

The church bells of the nearby Bogoylavansky Cathedral rang out and brought my attention away from the burning flame into the home of Orthodox Christians here in Irkutsk. A church service was in progress on my arrival so I sat at the back of the church on a wooden bench and observed the many Orthodox Christians worshipping their lord Jesus Christ. My attention was focussed upward at the ornate and colourful murals spread across the ceiling. Orthodox churches always look so ornamentally pleasing on the outside with their golden bauble and onion domes interwoven with their bright and distinct colours flanked upward by the double crosses of Orthodoxy. The inside of such churches are equally as eye-catching with their numerous golden icons spread all across the walls and each one depicting a scene and narrative from biblical history. The altar is a place of sanctity where only the priest dwells, as he is the physical representative of Jesus in his home. The Orthodox priest is a man of solemnity and of strength. He is physically imposing with his long and colourful garments and his dark beard. All prayers are sung and there is a luscious lyricism to the soft chanting when combined with both the priest and his followers. The doors to the altar are golden and one can briefly catch sight of the marble altar where the body and blood of Jesus is blessed in order to distribute to the believers. I saw many young children and how observant they were beside their families. They continuously look at their parents and follow their bowing in submission and making the sign of the cross from right to left. After the service, the priest came down amongst the people to bless them individually. Each child received a small and oval shaped piece of blessed bread. Everybody seems to know one another and there is a sense that the people are more like a family and an inner connection exists that is natural in such peaceful places. I really admire how services are carried out in Russian Orthodox Churches throughout the world. It brings me back in my mind to moments when I used to attend such services. I am alone in these churches now but in the past I was standing next to her as we would attend services together as a couple. How I long to replicate those moments and to have them back in the present but no miracle will be granted for me. All I do now is wander in and out of these churches and I sit alone usually on a small wooden bench at the back of the church. I pray for a while and I think for even longer. I just like to sit in silence and listen to the wisdom that resides in the space beyond. I am obscure here; nobody knows me. I just exist in my own internal self.

Of all Russian stories it is that of the Decembrists that is both the most heroic and the most romantic. These Russian soldiers who were once loyal to the tsar but then staged a coup to overthrow Romanov rule in Russia on 25 December 1825. Their coup failed miserably in St Petersburg. Some of them were killed by firing squad but the majority of the soldiers were punished and sent to exile in Siberian prison camps in Chita. The story becomes romantic when the wives of the exiled husbands followed them across Russia to Chita. Two wives, in particular, have become synonymous with romantic Russian ideology. They were Maria Volkonsky and Yekaterina Trubetskaya. These faithful Decembrist wives gave up their whole lives in St Petersburg and Moscow to live in exile for over two decades in Siberia where they helped set up schools, hospitals and edited newspapers, all with one aim to champion the rights of their beloved husbands.

I walked along the Maria Volkonsky and Trubetskaya house museums that are located close to each other in old Irkutsk. These traditional wooden Siberian homes with their elegant windows and shutters stand in testimony for the heroic bravery of Russian women. Russia is often referred to in matriarchal terms as mother Russia due to the devotion and honour played by its women in times of great suffering.

Instead of languishing at home and saying goodbye forever to their husbands, they decided at the centre of all true heroism is the courage to act and act decisively. The wives would not give up on their husbands because they were a part of them and a part of their family. The bravery carried out by these faithful wives was the impetus needed to further inspire their husbands to not give up on themselves because they were not alone in their struggle.

It is very interesting that the Decembrists staged a coup to overthrow Tsar Nicholas the first in 1825 as it was ninety-two-years later during the Russian Revolution that Tsar Nicholas the second and his family were murdered by the Bolsheviks and that event ended 300 years of Romanov rule in Russia. The Decembrists continue to be admired and remembered in Russia even though their coup ended in failure. Perhaps the Bolsheviks learned from the Decembrists that a plot to overthrow tsarist rule in Russia would be possible with careful and strategic planning.

I walked down Dekabrshkikh Sobytiy Street in old Irkutsk. For me, this is the most refined street in all of Irkutsk. It's architectural homes stand in testimony to a traditional Siberian way of life in the 19th century. Each home along this tree-lined street, although decaying with the erosion and passage of time depict structures that stand proud and heroic in modern times as a beacon of hope from a traditional way of life that worked together with the natural resources of Siberia. Each home is different to the next and what is often depicted is the personality of the inhabitants within. There are both one and two-story homes and some are built using only the original wood without any colour. The colour on such homes is used sparingly as a striking blue or deep green along their windows and shutters. Other homes are colourfully decorated in its wood along the windows, shutters and doors. I passed by a wooden home where an old lady opened the long shutter window, which provided a short glimpse into her world. The planks of wood are positioned horizontally on top of each other and often the roofs of these homes have a distinctively darker wood to differentiate it from the rest of the home. I came upon a two-story home that used both green and blue window shutters to capture a most genteel and pleasing home.

Outside the entrance to 130 Street and a perfect place to rest after my walk-through old Irkutsk is beside the bronzed statue of Babr. This hybrid Siberian tiger with a beaver's tail and paws stands alert with a sable in its mouth and is proud as the symbol of Irkutsk in welcoming all to 130 Street by touching his right paw to bring good luck. On this very warm Sunday afternoon in Siberia, I am so far away from home but sitting and watching young couples stare into each other's eyes in moments of requited love I might as well be in any park in Europe as human behaviour and interconnectivity remains omnipresent.

Although my legs were heavy after the walk through Irkutsk, I pushed on and followed in the direction of the sun as my stomach began to rumble. It would be my final meal in Irkutsk before my departure for Omsk. I came upon a restaurant along the main street and entered its very large and wide door. I headed directly for the corner of the restaurant just like I usually do when going out for a meal, as I like to position myself next to a window with a full view of the open restaurant and to the world outside.

I was the only customer on this Sunday afternoon and I immediately ordered a bowl of mushroom soup with a main course of risotto along with a freshly squeezed apple juice. I took out my journal and pen and was about to reflect on my experiences in Irkutsk and Lake Baikal over the last few days when I heard a male voice coming from the direction of the kitchen which said, 'You are a long way from home,' the tone grew louder as the chef walked towards me.

'Yes I am.'

'Are you from the UK?' he asked.

'No, I am from Ireland.'

'What are you doing in Siberia?' a curious chef inquired.

'I am crossing Russia by train along the Trans-Siberian Railway from Vladivostok to Moscow,' I proudly replied.

'Crossing Russia by train?' a bewildered chef asked.

'Yes,' I smiled in reply.

'But why not fly?' a puzzled chef asked.

'I wanted to experience the real Russia by crossing its landmass.'

'Russia does not have a lot for tourists to see,' echoed the chef.

'Well, Russia is the largest country in the world with a long history and a diverse nature. I think there a few things to grab the attention of a visitor here,' I sarcastically replied.

'Where are you from?' I asked with an attempt to divert the negative energy that was beginning to form in the restaurant.

'I was born in Belgrade Serbia,' the chef replied.

'I visited Belgrade once in the winter when it was snowing,' I replied.

'I returned to the Balkans last summer for a month. I really love the diversity of cultures there,' I stated.

'My favourite place in the Balkans was Kosovo,' I replied with nostalgia in my eyes.

'Kosovo is Serbia and Serbia will always be part of Kosovo,' stated the chef with a determined and raised tone to his voice.

'Kosovo suffered so much during the Balkans War but isn't it better now that there is peace there?' I asked the chef.

'No,' an angry chef retorted.

'The Albanians have destroyed our Kosovo and tried to erase our history and culture,' said the chef.

Isn't it terrible how we all live in a world that is dominated with nationalism? Why does it have to matter so much our ethnicity? Shouldn't it matter more about who we are as a person and how we should find a common ground on which to unite and not such a divisive element that ultimately keeps us apart?

Militant nationalism coupled with a fundamental ideology are the key components that spark the fires to a division amongst cultures that end on the battlefield with the bloodshed of man. When we act with such anger and vitriol towards our fellow man, we begin to sow the seeds of division that lead to wars and such atrocities like those that occurred in the Balkans of the 1990s. It was at that moment as the waitress entered from the kitchen to bring my mushroom soup and juice that I took my leave and went to the bathroom to wash my hands.

As I turned on the cold water tap, I immediately began to regret my decision to enter this restaurant. I stared at the reflection in the mirror. Who is this man that stares back at me? I have become so old now. My hairline has receded, the lines along my forehead are crevice like and numerous. The eyes are sad and forlorn. Long gone are the days when I was youthful and happy. The ageing process has entered and took possession of me and will not depart until my days are over. There is no way to fight it. I must accept my eventual fate. Life passes by so quickly. We wake up in a haze and suddenly twenty years have gone by and this once young boy has now become an older man. Is he wiser? Is he happier? The eyes are still the same. They don't age. They remain constant and alert but surrounded by the inequities of our lives.

I returned in silence to my table as the aroma of the thick mushroom soup greeted my presence. No matter what happens, the writer will always revert to the internal world where the surroundings are safe and akin to the world that he belongs too.

There was a price more than a monetary value that I had to pay in order to enjoy such delicious food in the comfort of that restaurant. It was the price of listening and witnessing to such negative energy coming from the chef. There was some brief respite as he prepared and delivered my risotto but I knew it would not be long before he returned to my table. I was the only patron and I was also a tourist so it was inevitable that my space would be disturbed once more.

'What part of Kosovo did you visit?' the chef asked.

'I visited and stayed in Prizren for three nights,' I replied.

'Prizren is overrun with Muslims now,' the chef replied.

'I really liked it there and the diversity of culture is something that really pleases me whenever I visit some new place,' I replied.

'Kosovo is the sacred heart of all of Serbia,' the chef exclaimed.

'Our history, our culture, resides there. All Serbian people know about the Battle of Kosovo in 1389 and the defeat of our Serbian King Lazar. Our Serbian people fought against the tyranny of Islam and the Ottoman Empire. You see, we will never relinquish Kosovo. We cannot let it go because we are part of the soil of Kosovo,' a passionate chef said.

'I understand such sentiments,' I replied back to diffuse such a negative tone. 'I live on a divided island where Northern Ireland is controlled and governed by the UK. I would love for the full island of Ireland to return to my country but I also realise that many British people call Northern Ireland their home so they have every right to live there in peace,' I replied.

'Kosovo was and will always be Serbian land. The Serbian people will one day take this land back and be reunited as a country once again,' an ominous tone came from the chef.

'Nothing is worth the pain, destruction and loss of life that took place during the Balkans War,' I said in reply.

'Serbia had to exert their will because our people reside in Bosnia, Croatia and Kosovo,' the chef said.

'Nationalism is the greatest fallacy ever inflicted on a people. Nothing of good ever comes from countries and peoples fighting. We should just all try and get along and live in peace surrounded by one another and our unique cultures,' I said.

'That will never happen,' replied the chef.

'The Serbian people are Orthodox Christians and are very different from the Muslim Albanians. We have nothing in common. We are more divided than ever united. We don't trust them and they don't trust us either. Peace is an impossibility in Kosovo until our sacred land returns to our people,' an ever more impassioned chef said.

As I sat there at the table alone enjoying the rest of my risotto, I began to think about how in this world of nationalism we mostly have problems with the people that are geographically closest to us. In Ireland, we do not have any political issues with Russia or Serbia because these nations are far away. Often our political issues lay with our closest neighbour, the United Kingdom and I am sure the United Kingdom would mention Ireland as a stumbling block for them too.

History has proven to us how often our fiercest enemy is the nation that is our neighbour. China and Japan have a history of conflict as does India and Pakistan and nations have broken apart such as North and South Korea. We mostly fear what is right in front of our own eyes but within such fear it is ourselves whom we cannot trust and so instead of acknowledging such distrust we go on the offensive to attack and such attack is carried out to our neighbours as somehow we believe that such attack will solve the problems that lay within our own misguided and nationalistic psyche.

I stumbled out from that restaurant with my stomach satisfied and filled but with a fog of apathy following me close behind. How can a soul that was illuminated and rejuvenated upon witnessing Lake Baikal a mere twenty-four hours ago be now reduced to a stigmatic volcanic eruption that knows no bounds or limitations? My weary legs walked the streets of Irkutsk one final time. There was a hunger in me akin to that of Hamsun's protagonist walking the streets of Christiania but my hunger is not a physical one. I am not hungry for fuel. I am hungry to challenge the deranged nature of our lives. I am hungry for a truth that I can see and almost touch but it remains forever distant due to that black hole of division that tries to ravage our mortal soul and transport us into the abyss of nothingness.

I sat on a bench in Kirov Square under the numerous fir trees beside the water fountain, soaking up the last rays of the sun as it was setting on yet another day in Irkutsk. The long flowerbed all around was a bounty of tantalising and aromatic colours of passionate red, gentle lilac, deep green and a golden fusion of yellow and white flowers all connected and surrounded with each other. There is an energy and quality to Kirov Square, which to me feels more like a park than a square.

I really admire how clean Kirov Square is. The people of Irkutsk really take pride in their city and this park epitomises the gentle nature and quiet environs that radiates to the city beyond. Kirov Square is the perfect setting for a quiet and reflective thought on the day that has just passed or for the days that are yet to come. The people of Irkutsk are so lucky and yet I am sure they are aware of this because they have Lake Baikal and the Taiga forest to be seduced by. They have the Angara River to admire and they have Kirov Square just simply to spend time in. Irkutsk is not Moscow nor is it St Petersburg, but in this part of Siberia, Irkutsk is nature's harmony.

Kirov Square is the perfect place in Irkutsk to come and admire the sensual beauty of Slavic women. I have noticed that these Slavic women generally come to this square as a couple to sit on the wooden benches for a while with their slender legs crossed and the immaculate look that greets me from across the square. When I observe such soft and feminine creatures, I revert into a shell of shyness and passivity. I fall upon their spell of inimitable beauty and the toxic masculinity that masks my shell surrenders accordingly. When I look upon the female, I am reminded of the ignominious brutality of the male. It is the male of the species who create nation states on which to divide, conquer by means of war. It is the male gender who fuelled by testosterone filled bodies who seek out the vulnerable, the quiet, the meek, the passive, the humble and who crushes such gentleness and forever renders the world with a never-ending broken line of blood spilled throughout our lands. The female carries the male into the world and raises him from a boy into a man but along the way it is the propaganda of paranoia and division that lures the male away from the fields full of corn to lands that wallow in the degradation of our own misery and depravity. Perhaps

Simone de Beauvoir was correct in her assertion that the female is indeed the second sex and it is so because of the violent dominance used and perpetuated by the male onto the gentle female.

I lingered that little bit longer at those as I was enchanted by all the sensuousness that surrounded me on this quiet evening along the Angara. My attention was drawn to one of them, as her image and the proportion in form reminded me of someone very special but very far from me. The long blonde hair became golden as the rays of the sun overhead sprinkled down upon her. Her skin was soft and almost porcelain like. Her cheekbones were high and protruding along her elegant face that was sparkling by the wide smile that began to melt my heart. Her eyes were a cerulean blue, like a full creation from the sky overhead. They sparkled and lived with an energy that was calling out for the truth that I so desperately seek. She wore a soft beige and short dress with speckles of yellow and pink flowers falling along the hem of her dress. I followed her long and tanned legs all the way down as the journey became fused and locked into the mystery of this woman I was fixated upon. I finally reached her arched ankles with the straps of her brown wedge heels surrounding them. She wore a violet colour polish to her soft toes that rested upon her still feet. She looked like her; she dressed like her. The deep and mysterious symmetry of this Slavic woman reminded me of her but then I fell out of the lurid mystery that I had fallen into and opened my eyes upon the reality that I was part of. It was not her and I knew she could be the most celestial creature in this world, a goddess from the cradle of humanity, an angel sent from heaven to greet me personally and yet I would only think of her, my own beautiful, my own fair, my own Slavic woman.

Where are you now, my great love and why do I sit here all alone with only my thoughts and despair at what we once shared but what is now in demise? Everywhere that I stand and everywhere that I sit there is that vacant space next to myself that was once inhabited by you my love but now it is occupied solely by emptiness, by the abyss of my broken and stolen dreams. I wonder, have you ever visited Irkutsk and rested upon this bench that I dwell upon at this moment? If I reach out for long enough, perhaps the memory of you will fall and rest on me like a shadow that I carry with me throughout all of these days and nights that I have counted since you departed my life. The two Slavic women across from me are oblivious to the loneliness that I feel every day without you, my dear. They don't know me and they don't know the life that we shared together.

They are immersed into the lives that they live and yet they are a witness to me as a living being sitting alone and dreaming of the magical to cascade from the heavens and sit next to me at this moment. How can I go on and live a life without you next to me, my love? I cannot recall a time in my life that I did not know you. I can indeed remember as a boy when I did not know you, but the problem is that when I think back to such moments, I can only think and transport myself from the present time and the feelings that are part of my mind and my imagination. There is a part of me that wants to erase you and all traces of you from my existence. He seeks a new life and a new love separate from you but even if he wins this battle of the duality of life within me, the memory of you will always endure like a burning candle fading from existence. The other part of me chooses to remember you and not to erase you from my thoughts and memories. If I were to erase you and forget you ever existed, then what was the meaning of the life that we once shared together? Perhaps you do not exist at all and I simply conjured you up from the eternal fields of roses within my imagination. How can I know for sure that you existed, my great love? My rational mind confirms that you indeed were real. My conscience reminds me that you did exist and the empty spaces that continue to reside where you once walked upon constantly remind me of the loss that I have inherited for a reason that has never been made known to me. If I knew and had assurances that you would return to me, I would wait both patiently and with love in my heart for a reunion of two individual beings who were once a single entity of love. I would wait a hundred years for you, my dear and fight the darkness within to cheat my physical death in order to fulfil that promise to reunite with you. I would physically grow older but a strength would grow within me if I knew that you would return. If Kirov Square was our chosen place of reuniting, then I would return here each day of the year in preparation for that desired meeting. Summer will end and as the leaves fall for the invitation of autumn, I would be here, my love, sitting alone on this bench as I am right now. The faces of the visitors would change with the passing of days but my love would never change. It would stay alive and fight for you, my dear. When the coldness of winter would enter as the blanket of snow would cover this park, I would still come and wait patiently for you, my love. No force of nature would dare to stop or prevent me from coming in to greet you. The ferocious coldness within the air would only be matched by the warmth of my heart that you inhabit and rest next to me. When the long winter would finally end, the promise of spring would arrive as the leaves would return from their hibernation and the flowers emerge with the poise, with the elegance, with the aroma of something special and fleeting about to happen. The sun would set on a new morning in Irkutsk over Kirov Square for the anticipated arrival of a very special guest. I would arrive early with freshly picked lilies and my shoes polished and sit on this bench that I have sat on for many a day with the hope of my dreams being fulfilled. And then, I sit and wait. I remain in silence like I always am but thinking about you and what you may look like now after so long being apart. I continue to wait and wait and wait and wait some more. The potential moment of reunification is severed with a return to my every day and ordinary and lonely existence. The two young Slavic women have by now left Kirov Square and another bench becomes unoccupied and lonely. As I departed Kirov Square for the final time I looked up as the sun was going down on the horizon and I realised that my love is farther away than she ever has been. The reality of my life and my loss crushes yet another decisive blow onto my dreams.

Chapter 14
Farewell Irkutsk

My departure from Irkutsk was in the darkness of a summer's night. A taxi collected me at 02:30 and brought me the short distance to the train station. I was only charged 150 roubles. It was the very same price that I was charged on Saturday when I went from Hotel Empire to the bus station. I saw the taxi driver key in 150 into his meter and the meter never changed throughout the journey. I can conclude, therefore, that 150 roubles is the standard fare for all local journeys such as going to either the bus or train stations. The taxi driver who brought me from Irkutsk train station to Hotel Empire last Thursday upon my arrival into Irkutsk charged me 500 roubles but he originally wanted to charge me 1000 roubles, which is almost ten times the standard fare. I arrived into carriage 10 of the 99 number train at 03:07. I stayed in another four bedded kupe and I had a bottom bunk with bed number 15.

When I arrived in the kupe, there were already two passengers occupying the upper and lower beds to my left and my bed 15 was on the lower right. I know the drill by now and I quickly put the sheets onto my bed and placed my suitcase underneath my bunk. Another passenger entered our kupe soon after and he occupied the final vacant bed at number 16. It doesn't take a passenger long to fit back into life onboard a Trans-Siberian rail journey. It was a farewell to Irkutsk as we continued westward through Siberia and onto Omsk.

The journey was twenty-six hours but with two extra hours as we passed two further time zones going back west, which made it a 28 hour journey before the arrival into Omsk tomorrow evening at 17:42. As I laid back onto my bed and listened to the constant chug of the 99 train moving forward, such a calming sound was disrupted by the loud and varied snores of my fellow passengers.

I have almost reached the halfway point on my journey across Russia. So much has happened since I departed Vladivostok but I am very eager for everything that is to come as I move into western Siberia and then depart Siberia and Asia for the Urals and Yekaterinburg before finally arriving into Moscow for my journey's end.

A new day arrived as I sat in the restaurant carriage looking out at the seemingly endless flow of Taiga forest. Dark clouds gathered overhead, which was a contrast to the warm days and clear blue skies that were spent in Ulan-Ude and Irkutsk over the past week. I tucked into a sumptuous vegetarian lunch of potatoes, mushrooms and onions with two slices of brown bread and a glass of apple juice. I much prefer this food to the instant noodles that many of my fellow passengers consume along the journey. Perhaps I am anti-social today but there are too many distractions in my kupe to read, write and to observe the outside world from my window as my cabin companions are constantly talking on their phones or watching YouTube videos without the use of headphones. I am sure it would be even worse if I spoke Russian as I would be able to understand all of their conversations but it is really annoying having to listen to conversations in such an enclosed space. Why don't they go outside into the corridor to speak in private? Another passenger is watching YouTube videos without the use of headphones and the rest of the kupe passengers can hear everything. Why doesn't he use headphones so that he can watch the videos in private? I wonder, do we ever consider about how other people feel in such situations? Technology takes us into other worlds but what is wrong with the world that is right in front of us? My phone is switched off during my days on the train. I have no use for it here. I only switch it on at night while I sleep so I can keep track of the time when I wake.

We passed a time zone at Reshoty Station and are now 4453km from and only four hours ahead of Moscow. I began this train journey at seven hours ahead of Moscow and it has been slowly reducing until we will pass the Urals next week and then we will finally make parity with Moscow. The town of Tayset at 4516km from Moscow, is located at the junction of the Trans-Siberian and Baikal Amur mainline railways. Tayset is notorious in Soviet gulag literature as it was used as a transit camp where prisoners were sent from all over the Soviet Union to the dreaded east which might as well have been to the end of the world for such prisoners as they became slaves and were worked to death under Stalin's tyrannical regime.

As I looked at such an expanse of space into Siberia, I began to question at what cost such a historical railway was built when thousands of the empire's citizens were used and then cast aside and forgotten as though they never even existed. To make matters even worse, the revolution was supposed to bring an end to such injustices imposed on its people by the empire but the Soviet Union carried out a systematic approach on dissidents by enslaving them in gulags throughout Siberia. The men who were worked to death and murdered away from their families were the real heroes from the Soviet Union.

One of the great pleasures of long journey's whether they be by land, sea or air, is those quiet moments spent reading. The present world continues with its everyday characteristics but there is another world present within the pages of a book and our present world becomes even more captivating by the heroism, inspiration and wisdom that each word conveys by the pen of its author.

I chose just two books to re-read but the books I chose in advance are synonymous with Russia, Siberia and one of them with the Trans-Siberian Railway. The books I chose are *Notes from the House of the Dead* by Fyodor Dostoyevsky and *Dr Zhivago* by Boris Pasternak. I chose Dostoyevsky's brutal and realistic portrayal of the barbarity inflicted onto humanity by an imperial regime because the land and its environment where Dostoyevsky was imprisoned for four years is my next stop, Omsk. The Trans-Siberian Railway becomes a witness for Pasternak's visual expanse of prose infused into his heroic characters as they question the bloodshed of the Russian revolt and a hint of something that is forever more intense and lasting than a civil war, love.

I met a French guy named Fabio and his girlfriend by the samovar. They are staying in carriage 10. They are from Bordeaux and for the last eight months they have been travelling through Asia and in particular Vietnam, Cambodia, Thailand, Laos, Myanmar, Malaysia and then onto China. The final leg of their journey is a seven-night Trans-Siberian Railway odyssey from Vladivostok to Moscow in one journey. Fabio told me that it is the first time as a couple that they have travelled together. They have been travelling ever since they left home late last year and this journey is a culmination of all their experience over that time before they reach the edge of Europe in a few days. When they finally arrive at Yaroslavsky Station, they will take a flight to Amsterdam, where they will complete their journey and relax for a few days before their arrival home to the south of France. They have fully settled into their seven night's journey west as they treat the train and their cabin as home. Fabio is dressed in pyjama bottoms, a t-shirt and slippers as he greets our providnitsa with a wide smile. I admire how this young couple did not fly home directly from China but instead carried on with their long journey home by crossing the largest country in the world by train. They will have such diverse memories to recall in the years to come of southeast Asia, China, the Russian far east, Siberia and finally western Russia.

I returned to my kupe for the last few hours before my arrival into Omsk. It was the first time throughout my Trans-Siberian Railway journey that I had the whole kupe to myself and what a lovely feeling it was to experience the rarity of silence. I looked out onto the idyllic scenery from my window without the interference of mobile phone conversations or the constant barrage of music hitting the walls of our small kupe. This was how train travel should be experienced because the solitude within the silence encapsulates the musical rhythm of the moving train with the panoramic view of the natural world externally. It will not last, of course, as I will arrive into Omsk Station at 17:42 and once more the silence will disappear into that chasm of the kupe as I move to the sounds of the outside world.

Chapter 15
Omsk

I am staying in the aptly named Tourist Hotel here in Omsk which is situated along the banks of the Irtysh River. Its grand size reminds me of the Buryatia Hotel in Ulan-Ude. The Tourist Hotel has eleven floors and I am staying in room 908 on the ninth floor overlooking the Irtysh River. A lapse in concentration allowed the taxi driver to charge me 1500 roubles for the journey to the Tourist Hotel. I promised myself never to be scammed again like I was when I arrived in Belgrade on 1 January 2015 but it did happen again as I let my guard down temporarily.

After I unpacked my suitcase, I came out to explore the streets of Omsk. One of the great feelings of travel is the arrival into a new city or town and especially those moments that a traveller exits the hotel to explore its new surroundings. There is such a curious anticipation of what lies ahead because everything is new, untouched and ready to be explored. Omsk is divided into two main parts. There is the north part along the Om River and the southern part along the Irtysh River. The Tourist Hotel is situated along the very tip of the southern side, with just a short walk over the bridge in order to navigate the northern side.

As I walked the busy streets of Omsk, I watched the sun going down along the far side of the Irtysh River. My first impression of Omsk is that it is a very clean city at least that was the impression that I got from these first moments in western Siberia. I really admire the architecture of the buildings along Ulitsa Lenin. Its diversity of colours shine ever so brightly with the sun's rays falling upon their roof tops.

I saw many people out walking the streets at the end of spring as they eagerly await the arrival of summer. Russia and in particular Siberia, is the land of extreme weather patterns. They experience very long and harsh winters but the arrival of spring with the blooming of its meadows heralds in seasons of light and heat that bring a direct contrast from the preceding seasons.

The traveller is always a hidden entity, as his footsteps gently trace the pavements of these new surroundings. Nobody knows the traveller here. He is just another face within the crowds as his nomadic ways guides him from one place to another but none of these nomadic lands will ever be home. Each new surrounding is an adventure of exploration from the preceding lands. The traveller must never interfere with the lives of these local people. He is a voyeur of constant movement and stimulation and when his time is complete, he must depart these lands as quietly and as anonymously as he had entered.

When I was going to bed last night, I took a carton of pear juice and two packets of peanuts from the mini fridge in my room but this morning the mini fridge was restocked for free by a lady who brought a trolley into my room with new refreshments. This might not sound news worthy for other tourists but it was something completely new for me since in the past I have always been charged when taking any goods from a mini fridge. For me, this adds such a touch of class and sophistication for the Tourist Hotel. The mini fridge is one of the great temptations for any guest in a hotel room. The guest is aware that when they retreat to their room at night that at any moment they can give in to their pangs of hunger and thirst in order to raid the mini fridge and consume their contents in the comfort and safety of their room. However, there is a cost always to be paid for such indulgence as the hotel staff are always watching and will count what goods are taken from their fridge on a daily basis. The old adage of there is an exception to every rule fits perfectly here for the Tourist Hotel because instead of charging the tourist for using the contents of the mini fridge they reward such behaviour by restocking the mini fridge to capacity and so the guest like all good forms of classical conditioning will use the mini fridge again and again until he departs this special hotel.

The surprises continued to flow from the Tourist Hotel as the setting for breakfast was a special wing of the hotel located between floors one and two. It had the feel of a conference hall as I observed a stage next to the buffet spread. I filled my empty plate with rice, potatoes, vegetables along with a bowl of corn flakes, a glass of apple juice and a cappuccino. The seats were as comfortable as arm chairs and one could temporarily think that they were relaxing in their own dining room.

Hotel Tourist is very large and there was constantly a flow of people entering and exiting these dwellings. I mostly prefer small and quaint surroundings on my travels but I do enjoy the isolated feel that Hotel Tourist gifts the traveller.

I sat for a few moments beside the Lenin statue along Lenin Square. During my brief stay there, I observed a father walking hand in hand with his young son and the little boy placed a bouquet of lilies at the feet of Lenin. This sense of patriotism astounded me. I wonder what words the father used to describe Lenin but in any case this young boy will grow to love, respect and, most of all, to honour mother Russia. There is a war memorial next to Lenin and such elegant and reflective places to Russia's heroic citizens can be seen across this large nation. Russia's present will not be able to ignore their bloody and heroic past because such bloody and heroic past forms our present too.

My primary reason for disembarking the 99 train at Omsk Station was to visit a literary museum to specifically trace the steps made by Dostoyevsky as he was sentenced to four years hard labour here in Omsk. A secondary reason for visiting Omsk was to spend time at the statue dedicated to the lovers as they stare into each other's eyes at a bench in the shade of the fir trees close to the Om River.

Upon my arrival at the bench of the lovers, I sat down next to the man and observed his amorous glance towards the woman. These lovers could be surrounded by a million people and yet they will only have eyes for each other. It was at that moment that I thought about her and a sadness enveloped me. I was thousands of kilometres from home and yet in an instant she invaded my thoughts. Is it the sight of these ageless lovers that has captured my heart and rendered me passive? I took out my journal and pen and I began to write her a letter from afar.

Wednesday, 29 May 2019,
Omsk, Western Siberia,
Russia.
18:08

My Dear N,

We go about our everyday lives in a flurry of activities and a chain of mundane and inconsequential thoughts easily forgotten in the past but thoughts of you can never be forgotten, can never be erased. They form the conscious, unconscious and subconscious thoughts within that sphere of delightful images.

I sit here next to a bronzed statue of a couple of lovers frozen in time and forever capturing the essence of what binds them together.

I am in the city of Omsk in Russia's western Siberia and this memorial to love has forced me to halt everything I am doing and just sit here to be surrounded by the immersion of love that exudes outward from this loving couple. The visitors come and go, day turns to night and the seasons change and yet the only constant that remains is the lovers together. The man has his left hand to a cup and the palm of his right hand is shown in mid-air as an indication of the conversation that these lovers were part of. The woman has both elbows on the table with her two hands joined together as she sits still with listening intent to her lover.

I wonder who this couple were and what were their everyday lives like? How fleeting all our lives are and we want them to last forever. All that remains of our lives are the small and all too brief moments that we shared together with one another. Our lives are a tapestry of numerous and forgotten moments eventually consigned to the past. It is only that grand memory box in our brain that can recall such moments. These lovers will not be forgotten. A brief and intimate moment from their life together has been captured still through the annals of time.

I sit here as a voyeur and unwelcome guest to these lovers. There is a sadness, a loneliness and a longing within my soul for what once was but for what will never be again. Who will build a statue for our love, my dear? Nobody! Who will remember the love that we shared with one another? Nobody! Our love died a long time ago and yet my heart continues to beat for you, to long for you. The rational part of me accepts the death of our love but that other part of me, the part that dreams of new horizons, of enduring love will never forget you and the spark of fire that you lit within my soul for those moments that we walked hand in hand on our journey together. I wonder where you are now, my love? Do you have any idea that at this very moment in a land far away on the other side of the world a young man is sitting ever so quietly and thinking of you?

If I had the gift to transport you to be sitting across from me now, we could become the physical embodiment of the lovers but I do not possess the powers of a magician. I am just a simple man whose heart longs and desires for a love that cannot resurrect itself and so all I am left with are those memories that we once shared together.

I really like Omsk N. There is something so elegant, so understated about this little gem in western Siberia. You would really love it here because it is so clean. The people of Omsk really take pride in their home and consequently the traveller must also take pride in this city as he walks its streets.

I have witnessed some beautiful churches on my travels but I think that today I set eyes on one of the most charming and harmoniously pleasing churches that I have ever seen, the truly awe-inspiring and captivating Holy Assumption Cathedral in the north of Omsk. Its setting is similar to Alexander Nevsky Cathedral in Sofia, in that it is built on a site adjacent to a road with traffic moving on all sides with a residential area of apartment blocks enjoying the panoramic view of this cathedral every day.

It is the delectable array of colours that captures the attention. There is a rich contrast between the large golden dome glistening under the sun and the smaller speckled turquoise domes standing on either side with finishing colours of pale red and white that gently calls on all visitors to come inside as the possibility of its majesty will not depart on entering its front door. Golden icons and an altar spread across on all sides greeted me as I entered such peaceful surroundings. No matter what a person's faith is, it is difficult to be unmoved when one lays eyes on such a sight.

In the afternoon, I took a gentle boat ride down from the Om River as it merged with the Irtysh River. I like the inconspicuous feeling such a scenic journey along a river brings. I thought about you N and imagined that you were here next to me as we would experience this journey together. I remember when we took a boat ride down the Seine River. It was many years ago but the sands of time never diminishes the special moments that we shared together. This is not Paris but it would be the whole world if you were here with me now.

It is time for me to say farewell N and let these lovers be alone together again. Tomorrow will be my final day in Omsk before I depart for Yekaterinburg beside the Urals. I am going to visit a literary museum which features an exhibit on Dostoyevsky who spent four years imprisoned in an Omsk gulag during his early life. Take good care of yourself and always remember that you are never truly alone in this world because there will always be one person who will be thinking of thee.

Ja Kachaju Ciabe my dear N,

Always,

D.

P.S. In the quiet moments of solitude, there rests a flickering light of hope that will guide us safely along our way.

D.

My final day in Omsk was dedicated to one of Russia's greatest writers. He was a man synonymous with great suffering and even greater humanity in both his real and fictional lives. He was a man that duly reacted to the circumstances in which he found himself to be in. The city of Omsk and the Siberian gulag will forever be etched into the consciousness of this man. His name is Fyodor Dostoyevsky. I walked up to the Dostoyevsky statue, who stands still in a grand pose dressed in his long coat with a book in his right hand. As I peered up at this great chronicler of psychological insight, I realised how very blemished and elusive all our lives are. Everything in our lives are random moments that cause a consequence and a reaction for the next moment in our lives until we reach the end and fade into the illusion of our earthly lives.

I walked across from the Dostoyevsky statue that led to a quaint park where I sat on a bench. Some pigeons came close to me and I began to feed them some bread leftover from breakfast. Why is it that of all the birds in the animal kingdom that it is the pigeon that is not afraid of humankind? Of course, the pigeon will rarely come alone. They are not a solitary bird. Perhaps it is the strength and concealment in numbers that allows such an interesting bird to continue to stand at the foot of man. The pigeon has quirky mannerisms. They walk around constantly bobbling their head and making bodily noises as they continue to seek out for nourishment. Why is it that man uses the derogatory phrase "pigeon brain" when referring to a lack of intelligence of a person? How can we possibly understand the brain of another species when it is our species that knowingly and intently takes the lives of our own species? It is our species that created the lives of Adolf Hitler and Joseph Stalin. It is our species that imprisoned the lives of Martin Luther King Junior and Nelson Mandela just because we decided to be divisive and to see one another as unequal. It was our species who burnt Joan of Arc at the stake and it was our species who created the extermination camps in Europe during the 20th century and murdered millions of innocent lives, all because we saw them as somehow unequal and inferior. We judge the pigeon for its brain but the pigeon simply lives, it breathes the air, it feeds off the earth and in the end it returns to the earth while the human continues to stain the earth with the blood of his own flesh.

It was then time to visit the literary museum and its exhibit on Fyodor Dostoyevsky. I was the sole visitor on this morning situated in a quiet and leavy street close to the Dostoyevsky statue. Omsk is a place that is synonymous with Dostoyevsky as he had to serve hard labour in a Siberian gulag for four years. From such hardships and almost death, those four years completely altered the life of the young Dostoyevsky and the spark of words that was lit inside his soul inspired Dostoyevysky to write *Notes from the House of the Dead*. The House of the Dead was where Dostoyevsky dwelt and he depicts in detail how life was for him and his comrades, of whom many succumbed to death due to the horrendous conditions, especially during the Siberian winters. At the exhibit, there was a photo of the mock execution that Dostoyevsky had to experience in St Petersburg and in the end their fate was four years imprisonment in Siberia.

If Dostoyevsky had been executed, the world would never have come to understand this man and his writing would never have existed. As I walked alongside images of Dostoyevsky, I pondered on how arbitrary all our lives really are. Human beings have the power to end the lives of other human beings in an instant and often there is nothing we can do to stop such a cruel and unjust fate. How many people throughout history never got an opportunity to fulfil their talents and instead faded from life and died without ever having lived? The biggest destruction of mankind comes from humankind itself. If ever the world will cease to exist, the only collaborator will be ourselves as we continue to be a divisive figure on earth.

I got to see Dostoyevsky's handwriting with a copy of his contract of *Notes from the House of the Dead* on display. As readers, we mostly see the typed pages of a writer's words but when we catch a glimpse of their own handwriting, it brings us ever closer to the personality of the writer. In modern times, writers type words onto a colourless screen and often they become detached from such words but in times past writers such as Dostoyevsky used an ink pen to transcribe his inner thoughts onto a blank page that allowed the writer to create art from their imaginations and experiences.

I learned from the exhibit that Dostoyevsky made quite a few travels during his life and especially to Baden-Baden in Germany, where there was a spa and he went there to try and heal his ongoing illness and especially to heal his many epileptic fits. Dostoyevsky also made trips to Dresden and Berlin, to Basel and

Zurich in Switzerland, to Vienna in Austria, to Milan and Venice in Italy and to Paris in France.

Dostoyevsky was truly admired and appreciated in his own lifetime, as was indicated by a copy of his funeral photo from 1891. Crowds thronged the streets of St Petersburg to see his coffin pass them. That was Dostoyevsky's second death because his first death was his life in chains in a house of death. Whenever I hear critics talk about *Crime and Punishment* and *The Brothers Karamazov* and what changes they brought to literature I become frustrated because for me Dostoyevsky's *Notes from the House of the Dead* was the beginning of his new life out from the shadows of death from the Siberian gulag. It was here in Omsk and the four years of suffering that Dostoyevsky endured that stirred up in him the humanity that was required to go on and produce truly great works of literature that we know today. Just like Dostoyevsky, I too will depart Omsk but I will not be in chains. I will continue on my journey west across Russia as a free man.

I went for a stroll on my final evening in Omsk. I sat on a wall overlooking the Irtysh River as the sun was flickering down on top of the river's waters. I saw a man showing his son how to fish. It saddens me that people see fishing as a nice hobby and something to pass onto the next generation. I never felt that way about fishing. Everything about fishing disturbs me. The act of placing a man-made fishing rod into the water with a hook and bait at the end of the line in order to lure innocent fish into its catch says so much about humans and our depraved and cunning nature.

In contrast, I observed a young couple walking hand in hand along a sandy beach. They were having so much fun together from being in each other's company. At one moment, the young girl ran off along the sand and the young boy chased after her and then they embraced and kissed. I also observed them taking selfie photos of their special moments together with the River Irtysh as their background. They were oblivious to the fact that I was watching them. They only had eyes for each other. I wonder will their love endure and last the test of time? If I returned to Omsk in five or ten years, will this couple still be together or is their relationship doomed to fade and eventually break? Who knows, really? I would like to believe that their love will endure but I also know all too well about the harsh realities of relationships and how cruel and sudden the endings come. In the blink of an eye, the person whom we have loved who was once by our side is now no more and forever we walk the path alone. All of that doesn't matter now for this couple. They are simply living in the moment and not thinking about the future. Saturday will be 1 June and the beginning of summer here in Siberia. This couple will have the rest of a lovely and long summer to spend together. Nothing else should really matter.

Upon returning to my hotel room to pack, I took one final glance out onto the Irtysh River as the sun was setting over Omsk. Out of the corner of my eye, I noticed two young girls down below close to my hotel. They were both looking at one of the girl's phones and were in a conversation about what they were looking at. Aren't all our lives one big mystery? We are all mysterious beings carrying around within us our own deep feelings and secrets that lay hidden from view. We are the authors and producers of our own great story, the story and narration of our own life.

Chapter 16
Memories

Wherever we go in life, a part of us remains in that place we departed from. Of all the places I have visited along my journey across Russia, it was Omsk that left the biggest impression on me. The nomadic traveller must continue on his journey. There is a sadness that pervades my heart on departing places like Omsk because I know that I will probably never walk its streets again but still a piece of my heart and soul will be left behind here and whenever in the future thoughts of Siberia come to my mind the memories that I experienced here in Omsk will remain.

It is yet another day and another train ride crossing this land. For the 900km journey from Omsk in western Siberia to Yekaterinburg in the Urals, I am staying in carriage 8 and bed 11 of train number 139. The most surprising thing about this journey is that I had the entire kupe to myself. Since I arrived for the 05:55 train, there have been no other passengers come into my kupe and most of carriage 8 is unoccupied too.

There is a family next door and another family a couple of cabins down but apart from that all the cabins were empty. I think if you asked any train traveller about what are the moments that they enjoy the most when travelling I am sure they would answer that it is those quiet moments when a traveller is sitting and surveying the world outside of his window as the images come rolling into his mind continuously.

I do enjoy the random conversations that come with train travel but if I am truly honest, then I know that I am happiest when everything is quiet and only the propellers from this powerful machine can be heard as time passes in the stillness of our own unique experience. For me, this is the true meaning of living in the present moment. I sit in the silence of a train in Siberia moving westward towards the Urals and this is exactly where I want to be and exactly where I happen to be at this very moment in my life. So often in life, we are running around in confusion with the noisy embers of our own lives and the great irony is that in such moments we do not have a clue where we are going. We are like lost sheep walking aimlessly around in circles, never finding the centre point which reveals the true meaning of life. There is often an irrationality in numbers whereby we calculate our daily lives by the clock, we count the money that we both give and receive, appointments and deadlines need to be managed, mathematics is central to our external world and the functioning of our business and social lives but how do we calculate the value of our internal thoughts? Can we measure them? We are constantly surrounded by ourselves and the divisive nature that we force upon one another but when we are alone we are our greatest champion. We always seem to be going someplace in life but what does it all mean? Are we ever happy in those moments of movement? If we were aware that we only had twenty-four hours to live would we still be bothered with all those appointments and deadlines? Life moves inextricably onwards and time cannot be reasoned with. I want to live and breathe each moment of this journey because what price can one pay for one's own freedom? When we are alone we are never divisive because in our silence we rest within the medium of our own existence and we realise who we are and ultimately we become humble within our own brokenness. To sit in silence moving forward surrounded by the natural world and where my mind and soul are at one is a moment of temporary bliss.

It is at such moments of happiness that I think about her and even at such ambrosial moments they would be even more pleasing if she was sitting next to me now, as we would share such moments together like we once did all those years ago. I have wanted to make this journey across Russia ever since I was a young boy but I am making this journey now because there is a chasm of sadness and loneliness within my heart and in order to fight such loneliness I decided to go on a journey of a lifetime in order to try and begin living again like I once did. She is never too far away from me. Yes, physically, due to geography we are thousands of kilometres apart but to see her, all I have to do is to close my eyes and to breathe. There is a photograph I carry with me and it is always placed in my writing journal. It is an image of her and I captured and nostalgically illuminated through time and all I can see is the happiness etched along our faces as we stand side by side. I do not remember anything about that day in particular. It was probably unremarkable but when I look at this image of us taken as the cold winter sun cascaded onto the waters of the Claddagh with the family of swans contented in their elegance and beauty I am reminded once more of the suffering nature to all our lives. I lovingly lean upon her closed eyes as she embraces gently into my arms. I look at this image with both happiness and sadness. I am now in the future as I look back into the past but I cannot reach out to these lovers and tell them what lies ahead. They must face their fate and ultimately part.

My precious moments of nostalgia are interrupted with the sound of our providnitsa hoovering the long and narrow hallway in front of our cabins. I watched her as she went to work on the red-coloured rug by removing all dirt and stains left over from the passengers of carriage 8. It is an ideal time for such work as our carriage is devoid of passengers but the duties and work of our providnitsa never stops.

As I watched our providnitsa at work, I began thinking about what useful activity hoovering is for body and mind. The person hoovering is always moving and bending their body so it is a good workout but for me, it is the assistance it gives for our mind that is most beneficial. The act of hoovering is most interesting in that the rewards it gives to the individual are instantaneous due to the speckles of dirt being removed with a sheer force from this ever so noisy machine. In contrast, if we wash a floor or paint a door, it takes time for the effort to be rewarded but this does not apply to the act of hoovering. It sends immediate responses to the reward and pleasure centres in our brain and when completed, although tired, the person certainly can be content when inspecting their area of work to show that it is clean once more. Our providnitsa came into my cabin but because I am its only occupant I ensured that everything would be clean for my daily inspection. Perhaps if my cabin was farther down the carriage I would have more time to prepare for such a daily inspection but our providnitsa's chamber is directly next door and so no chances could be taken.

We stopped at Tyumen at 12:08 although my watch read 13:08 but since we passed another time zone, we move back one hour and now we are only two hours behind Moscow time. I stepped off the train at Tyumen to get some air and I sat on a bench near the platform. Tyumen is Siberia's oldest town and was founded in 1586. Before the revolution, many convicts passed through Tyumen on their way to the gulags of Siberia. I began to recall those old photos of Dostoyevsky on the walls of the literary museum at Omsk. Dostoyevsky passed through Tyumen along with his fellow convicts as they made their way slowly to Omsk. Their freedom was cruelly taken from them by their own people and here I am at the edge of Siberia, sitting outside drinking iced tea as a free man. Nobody is going to take me away in chains and force me into the House of the Dead. The only chains that are around me are the chains of my own indecisiveness. After departing Tyumen, we soon passed the town of Siberia which is the frontier between the Urals and the region of Siberia. Siberia is located at 2102km from Moscow and I now said a fond farewell to Siberia which has been my home for the last ten days.

I am sad to leave Siberia which is as wild, as untouched, as untamed and as free a place that I have ever set eyes upon before. Why is it that the first word a person thinks about when they hear the word Siberia is cold? Yes, of course this region has harsh winters but its summers are a testimony to the natural world it resides within. Its natural environment inhales and exhales the oxygen from their ever widening and strong lungs. The traveller who passes through Siberia is that much more wiser, that much more humble, to have experienced such nature for a brief moment of his life. When the traveller will experience the natural world of other places in the future, he will always contrast those places with the time he spent within Siberia. Siberia has passed now but we are still in Asia geographically as the official Europe-Asia border is located at 1777km from Moscow and a mere 39km away from my next destination, Yekaterinburg. For the next three nights, I will still be in Asia and will not officially arrive back into Europe until early on Monday morning when I depart Yekaterinburg for Moscow. As I sat down in my cabin with a warm coffee and some waffles my attention was drawn to life beyond the window. I noticed the changes that have been taken place in the natural environment. Gone are the expanses of Taiga forests with their innumerable Siberian pine and they have been replaced with tall evergreen trees that dot the landscape, as we are now in the Ural range of western Russia. Today is the final day of spring here in Russia and tomorrow will herald the beginning of summer.

As I looked down at my table at a copy of Pasternak's *Dr Zhivago,* I am reminded of what delights that would be seen if I had taken this long journey across Russia in the winter. There would be the endless snow of a Russian winter. The great characteristic for me of a Russian winter is its scintillating silence. People retreat indoors for warmth but those brave souls who venture out are rewarded with dazzling blankets of snow as the natural environment goes back into hibernation and what remains is the continuing empty void of silence. My experience to the Zhivago's is very different. They are heading away from

Moscow and into Siberia in winter, while I am beading away from Siberia and onto Moscow as summer arrives. There is still a connection between the fictional world of the Zhivago's and the real life of a traveller, as both rely on the power of the trains to cross this unbounded land. We are also both individuals who seek answers within our own humanity, as nihilism reverberates throughout our society and world.

When I departed Vladivostok two weeks ago, it was cold and foggy along the pacific but now over 7000km farther west, it is awash with natural colours all over the forest range. It is still a little overcast, as the strength of the sun has not reached down upon us yet.

My next destination is where the old aristocracy met a new ideology and such a meeting brought a most brutal revolution that ended with the barbaric murders of the Romanov family. Out of such violence came a new ideology for Russia when communism was born. This destination is Yekaterinburg and Russia's fourth largest city. I had been getting used to the pastoral vistas of Ulan-Ude, Irkutsk and Omsk but now a much larger city awaits me as we edge closer to Moscow and my journey's end.

I always enjoy the slow pace of a train as she glides effortlessly into a large city station. Yekaterinburg is a large and industrial city and its suburbs of high-rise apartment blocks become evident to me as the train slows gently. The next train I will take will be the final journey along the Trans-Siberian Railway bound for Moscow. The wild nature and its environment of Siberia has passed and now it is a return to industrialisation and man-made pollution.

I am really going to miss Siberia. I was unidentified there and yet so free and at one with the nature I shared a space with. In Siberia, I always felt that I was a guest who was invited into its paradise for just a short while on condition that I depart its land without ever interfering into its environment as quietly as I had entered.

The traveller on coming to a destination must be open to new experiences and not to judge its land or people on previous experiences or delusional expectations. It was time to exit carriage 8 of train number 139. I will be staying for the next three nights at the Trans Hotel on Gogolya Street in the centre of Yekaterinburg. So much has happened already over the last few weeks and now I have reached western Russia but the experiences that have yet to be lived will become evident to me as time will pass onwards.

Chapter 17
Yekaterinburg

Of all the subjects I studied at school, it was history that left the biggest impression on my young mind. I never saw history as simply the learning of facts, dates and inevitable battles off my heart. History, for me, was much more complex, much deeper and substantial than all of that. We carry the consequences of our historical past and our actions will determine the consequences for future history. The lives we live are the result of the historical actions of previous generations.

When I was at school, I always became excited with a glint in my eyes when the topic of Russia came into view. It was like I had been in darkness and suddenly the light was switched on and my attention was fervent. Our teachers would talk about Russia and its people as they were the other. They were seen as red, as communist and as bad. The textbooks that were supplied for us re-iterated such propaganda and so that is the way it remained until this young mind woke up from the foggy illusion of our own deep insecurities latent within our own historical propaganda that we had inherited from our own predecessors.

History cannot exist in such nothingness. It must first be understood with a universal neutrality. Our present lives must then be lived in such a manner that we have fully grasped our own history so that we can contribute to our future citizens. Before I was to read the stories of Tolstoy, Dostoyevsky and Chekhov, I was to learn about Ivan the Terrible, Rasputin, Lenin and Stalin. These names became fixed into my mind as I studied about the history of Russia. To fully know a people you cannot learn about them in a book. They are just facts told to us on paper but to truly understand a people, to empathise with them, to identify with them then we must leave behind our own inherited misconceptions and go to such lands to immerse ourselves into a culture in order to change who we are and what we are to become.

Of all the places I wanted to visit before I set out on my journey across Russia, it was here in Yekaterinburg that I felt compelled to visit and spend time in to try and grasp the historical significance of this place beside the Urals. It was here on the outskirts of Yekaterinburg and deep in the forests during the Russian Revolution that a heinous crime took place, which altered the course of Russian history. The murder of the Romanov family in Yekaterinburg and the disposal of their bodies permanently severed aristocracy in Russia by welcoming in a new way of life that was supposed to signify equality for all, communism.

It was the first day of summer in Russia with clear blue skies as the midday sun shone down on Yuri and I as we set out for Ganina Yama monastery situated 16km northeast of Yekaterinburg. Yuri works as a security guard at the Trans Hotel but is now doubling as my taxi driver to the sacred and hallowed site that is an integral place of visit in order to try and understand the complexities of the Russian Revolution.

I always like such private journeys to new lands as it gives me the opportunity to converse with local people in order to understand how they view history from the inside compared with my external view.

'Where have you come from?' an inquisitive Yuri asked.

'I began my journey three weeks ago in Vladivostok and slowly made my way by train across Russia,' I retorted.

'Why didn't you fly from Vladivostok to Yekaterinburg?' a puzzled Yuri replied.

'I wanted to see the real Russia and its people while travelling by train slowly westward,' I stated as Yuri and I looked towards each other.

'Did you see Siberia?' an excited Yuri asked.

'Yes, I did. I crossed it by train but made stops at Ulan-Ude, Irkutsk and Omsk,' I told my new Russian friend.

'Oh Irkutsk,' sounded Yuri. 'One day I will visit Irkutsk and see Baikal,' a passionate Yuri responded. 'My father used to tell me stories of Baikal before going to sleep as a boy,' a nostalgic Yuri said. 'I remember most of all when he would tell me about Rinka, the goddess of Baikal,' a passionate Yuri told me. 'You see, Rinka would rise out of the waters of Baikal at sunset to watch over her people,' a melancholic Yuri retorted.

'Will you go to Baikal with your father?' I asked.

'Niet,' replied a tearful Yuri. 'My father died in Irkutsk when I was ten years old but I made a promise to him that I will one day go to Irkutsk and walk along the shores of Baikal,' a determined Yuri echoed.

It was at that moment that I began to think about my own father and, just like Yuri, I too felt the void that exists after our father departs this world. Yuri and I were born into different nationalities. We speak different languages but we are more united than we are divided.

'Have you been to Ganina Yama before?' I asked Yuri curiously.

'Da, many times but I don't go there anymore,' a sad Yuri said.

'You see, the day that the Romanov family were murdered, Russia lost its soul,' a reflective Yuri stated. 'The old Rus was a golden land where our people worked, appreciated and loved our land but on that fateful night, mother Russia entered tyranny and she is yet to wake from her long sleep,' said Yuri.

As we arrived on the grounds of Ganina Yama, I said farewell to Yuri as I began to immerse my thoughts into what Yuri had said to me for those brief moments that we were together.

I walked under the large and numerous evergreen trees that surrounds the monastery on all sides. Seven wooden temples stand erect and were built to honour the seven members of the Romanov family, who in death will forever be remembered and honoured as martyrs. There are individual memorials to Tsar Nicholas, his wife Alexandra and a very moving memorial to all five children holding their crosses just like Jesus did on his walk to Calvary before his crucifixion.

I slowly made my way inside to both the Church in the Name of the Icon of the Mother of God and the Tsar Temple which is located on either side of the monument to the royal children. I observed the deferential obedience been given to the Romanov family in their death as pilgrims recognise that this family are now saints of the Russian Orthodox Church. I then walked over to the former mine shaft where the Romanov family were disposed of with the intention of erasing them from existence.

There is a wooden observation platform circling the former mine shaft and a Russian Orthodox cross standing in front of the pit. I stood there in the silence as my mind tried to comprehend the crime that took place here in 1918. This is a place of deep sorrow because one recognises that it was human beings who committed such a crime onto other human beings.

We continue to hurt one another throughout history in our attempt to destroy our humanity and existence. Every human being has a conscience and we also understand fear and pain. I cannot comprehend the terrible fear that went through the minds of the Romanov family before they were shot to death in Yekaterinburg. Their pain and earthly lives were over but the crime continued as their bodies were callously burnt and dumped here in a final act of vengeance onto aristocratic Russia. Surely, communism was doomed to fail with the blood of the Romanov family on their conscience and a stain on the Russian soul that cannot be removed.

The most important possession we hold is our humanity that shadows us throughout our earthly lives. No matter what our differences are, we must try and understand and respect each other as human beings. We should never attempt to commit such a crime against our own because when we attempt to destroy our own, we destroy the goodness of being human and then we are lost forever. We have a duty to stand against such crimes and to speak out against the suffering of all humans and animals. History is such an important part of our lives. We should learn and recognise our history in order to prevent similar crimes taking place during our present story.

I feel sad to be here at such a place of human suffering and tragedy because I realise what we are capable of as human beings in the destruction of each other. The imperturbable assuredness of this forest clearing in nature with the sun flickering through and the sweet sounds of the birds overhead cannot mask or alter the crimes that took place here in the depths of the soil at Ganina Yama. The blood that was spilled here was once compatible with human life. Only death through the implementation of murder by the aggressors onto the innocent exists deep within the earth of this land.

This is yet another grave that is scattered throughout the soil of the earth. where human beings violently ended the lives of other human beings. Is there ever an endpoint to the evil of our crimes?

As I stared down onto the blood stained earth, I am all too aware that as a human being I am capable of committing such crimes as much as I could have the life brutally taken from me. Is there any hope for us as a human species? The crime that took place here is over one hundred years old and nothing has really changed within the hearts of man. If the Romanov family could walk out from this pit and trace the last hundred years, they would learn about civil wars, revolutions, world wars, the Holocaust, man's ongoing and enduring war onto itself, communism, socialism, capitalism. They are all divisive as they pit human against human in a never-ending battle without a victor. Perhaps it was the gentle life and message of the Buddha under the tree contemplating his own existence and in the end realising that the answers to all our human questions lay internally and the message of one's life is the love that we give to all living beings whilst we breathe the air into our vulnerable human bodies.

I feel deep pathos for the Romanov children even though I never knew them in this life but they were forcibly prevented from reaching their full potential and never allowed to grow, to flourish, to love, to become parents by giving life into their offspring. The moralist within me knows that it is not for human beings to interfere or break the chain of humanity by taking the life of another being. When we take the life of another human being, it is not one life that we take or that we are responsible for. The life that was taken breaks the indelible link to its future offspring and an entire generation of lives will never live. By committing such a crime, we not only alter the present moment but our story, which will become history, is forever altered and distorted by our crimes onto one another.

As I departed Ganina Yama and took my seat on a bus back to Yekaterinburg, I am again reminded that I am alive, that I am a thinking and living being with blood running through my veins and a heart fighting for my life every second that I breathe in this life. As a thinking and rational being, I am also aware that one day my heart will stop beating, I will then breathe my last and my body will return to the earth just like that of the Romanov children. There is no hiding from the destruction of our humanity. We are a product of the stain from our birth that only ends with the destruction of ourselves.

The June sun shone down onto the deserted streets of Yekaterinburg on this Sunday morning. I like the disguised feel of a city or town that is afforded to a visitor. A traveller can tell much about a people when they are not there. We are often so busy looking at one another and the internal monologue that follows us throughout our lives but one of life's great pleasures are those quiet and ever so random moments that we get to experience wandering as a nomadic voyeur through the home of others.

I can tell a lot about a nation and its people by how clean their home is. When each individual deems oneself responsible for their home, then the work that is carried out becomes part of the collective just as was echoed by Lenin over a century ago. I observed the machine road sweepers as they went from street to street cleaning all remnants from last night's activities. When a traveller sees such pride in a people for their home, then as a consequence the traveller begins to live the very same ideal. It becomes a learned behaviour.

The feeling of desertion carried on from the breakfast table at the Trans Hotel where I was its sole guest. I briefly caught sight of Yuri but he didn't look my way as his attention was drawn towards the manager of the hotel. A traveller can quickly forget how when we are experiencing a new culture, the people that we come into contact with are living in the midst of their everyday lives with their own duties and responsibilities. The places that I experience here in Yekaterinburg are all new to me but to a local person they are experienced every day.

How quickly in life the resplendent can become the mundane. If you passed by an oak tree on your way to work each day, when do you begin to lose sight of that marvellous oak tree and not observe its branches and leaves once more? If something is always there, then do we not see it anymore? Do we take for granted the meaning of what it represents? Perhaps we are so consumed with our daily lives that the large oak tree becomes invisible by our own demise. However, if gold, diamonds and paper money were placed onto the branches would we suddenly stop at the oak tree?

The grace that surrounds us each day is as fleeting as the time we give to such grace. The street that I walked upon to get to and from my hotel is called Gogolya, named in honour of the great Ukrainian writer Nikolai Gogol. I feel at any moment that this quiet, unassuming and tree-lined street will suddenly come alive with the characters from Gogol's stories. If I close my eyes and open my imagination, then perhaps I will once again experience the adventures of Akakay Akaviench and Kovalev. I think we die a little each day by the sheer monotony and farcical element to our own existence but when we release our imagination and our creativity we slowly begin to live a little more and it is at those brief moments that we can catch sight of that old oak tree on our way to work.

I stopped to rest for a while beside the city pond. I sat on a bench with a warm coffee and from the corner of my eye a little boy dressed in navy dungarees, white runners with blond hair and holding a toy water boat said some words to me in Russian that I could not understand. I smiled at him in my ignorance as his father, who was also carrying a toy water boat, called his son to the edge of the pond. I have seen this game before from when I was at the Luxembourg Gardens in Paris. The aim of this simple game is to place one's toy water boat into the water and push it gently so that it will glide to the other side of the pond. The charm of such a game is how tense and exciting it is because one never knows who will win until the final moment as the boat disembarks on the far side. How special this game is for the young boy, as he is playing with his papa. The young boy screamed with excitement as his blue sail boat pushed off from the gentle waters. His loving and kind father waited a couple of moments to release his green coloured sail boat. The young boy is so excited that he wants to jump into the water following his boat. Instead, he raced to the north facing end of the pond to continue screaming his willingness for his blue boat to win the race between father and son.

As I watched such an intimate moment between father and son, I wondered to myself if ever in this lifetime I will become a father of my own and be able to experience such special games to play with my daughter or son? Am I destined to wander this earth as a nomadic voyeur but to do so alone within my own consciousness? When I was with her, we talked about the possibility of becoming a family and welcoming a child into this porous world. We even had a name already chosen if we were to be blessed with a son. We were to name him Vasily after her grandmother's son, who departed this world and left a bereft mother to bury his body back into the earth. The dream that we once had together ended with the death of our love. I wonder where she is now? I wish she was sitting next to me now and we could both be cheering for our daughter or son to win the boat race across the pond. She is not sitting with me now. She has not sat with me for a very long time. If I could reach out to her now, I would whisper into her soul that I love her, that I always love her. There is a sadness in the illusion of love. The sadness is the transient nature of all our lives. We hold on to the dream of the past like sunbeams reflecting and dancing onto radiant waters. My mind's attention followed the boy's shriek of euphoria as his blue sail boat finished first to win the race against his father.

I walked up to a little park and sat on a bench overlooking the Church of the Blood all glowing in white with its golden cupolas under the summer sun. I wanted these moments to be spent alone and in contemplation of the historical significance of the place that I will soon set foot within. If I was unaware of the events that took place in this building over a century ago, then surely my visit to this church would be like my visit to any other church on my travels. When we learn facts and can piece together events that coupled together lead to a story, then how we view such a place changes. Before this church was built, a great crime took place on this very site with the callous murders of the tsar, his wife and their five children. Their deaths were deliberate, cruel, slow and politically altering Russia's history.

Yesterday, I traced the events following such murders to the sacred site of Ganina Yama and today I set foot upon the place where the Romanov family last walked and breathed the air in this world. The Church of the Blood is positioned on an incline with steps on which to rise in order to enter this large and imposing structure as it looks down onto Yekaterinburg. I walked past the large murals of the Romanov family. The Russian Orthodox Church do not want people to forget what happened here in 1918 and how such an event ended aristocracy in Russia as communism swept to all parts of the Soviet Union following its brutal revolt.

When a person with whom we love dies in this life, whether it be unjustly or natural, we try to keep our memory of them alive with physical images of that person hauntingly still but forever beautiful across time. The person will not be forgotten and will live on through the deeds of the people who carry their memory forward.

When we look back and reflect on history through the prism of our present moments, we view such history differently. How can any sane and empathetic person see the shocking and bayonetting to death of five innocent children as an act of justice and necessary for the future of Russia and its people? When we take the life of a child, we permanently destroy the innocence within ourselves and we become the murderous act that we had instigated onto such innocence.

I then walked down to the basement and into the hallowed and consecrated site of the dead Romanov family. The basement was dim with a dark red colour along its walks to symbolise the red blood that was spilled so violently at this place in 1918. The First World War was coming to an end in Europe but Russia's war of communism was just beginning as a new era was brutally won by the Soviets.

The Romanov family have been elevated to sainthood by the Russian Orthodox Church. It disturbs me to witness the many murals on the walls of the church depicting the Romanov family as saints and welcomed into heaven. How do we know that the Romanov family are now saints in heaven? It is the Russian Orthodox Church here on Earth that have elevated them to saints but how can we possibly know and comprehend the place and position they now hold in another world? It makes no logical sense for human beings to make such statements of facts about other human beings when it is human beings who deliberately take the lives of one another. The only thing that we can be sure about and control in this life is how we treat one another by our actions. We have no comprehension or can alter nothing in another world due to the stain that rests forever within our own soul. Isn't it a falsity to presume such another life for this family when we cannot possibly know this with any certainty? What criteria does the Russian Orthodox Church use to decide who gets elevated to that of saints in another world? How come the Russian Orthodox Church has not elevated the over three hundred children that were murdered at a school in Beslan on 1 September 2004? Their lives were cut short too when they became the innocent victims to a harrowing siege lasting days. There was no church built on that site in Beslan where their young lives were taken. Not one of their lives have been elevated to sainthood. Is it, therefore, that the Romanov family have been elevated as saints not only because of how they were murdered but mostly because of the elite position they held in Russia before its revolution ended tsarist rule? Could a neutral observer therefore conclude that the Romanov family held a privileged life here on Earth and now they get to hold a privileged life in the next world? What is the message in all of this on which we can learn?

Chapter 18
Journey's End

It was a little after 09:00 on this Monday morning as I was awakened by the sounds of playful children as they entered and exited and entered again our kupe in carriage 10 of train number 99 as it moved westward from Yekaterinburg across the Urals to Moscow.

It was my fifth and final train journey along the Trans-Siberian Railway. One of the most pleasing aspects of travel are those unexpected moments when we share a space with people along a shared journey for some brief moments and one such moment occurred for me on the final leg of my journey to Moscow as I got to share a space with a family from Siberia. I shared our kupe with a father named Alexander and his two sons named Ivan and Nikita. A few cabins down were the rest of the family, which included Christina, the wife of Alexander and mother of Ivan and Nikita, along with their daughter Alyona and one-year-old son Makar. Travelling with them was also their friend Sasha who is from Vladivostok and he is travelling to Moscow alongside his father Oleg. When I heard the shouting and laughter, I thought that I was dreaming and back in Yekaterinburg along the pond watching the boat race between the father and son.

There was no point going back to sleep so I got up, made my bed, got dressed and went the short distance to the bathroom, passing the samovar and providnitsa's chamber. As I was looking upon my tired reflection in the mirror whilst brushing my teeth, I knew that soon my journey along this great railway will come to an end just like all great journeys must suddenly and naturally come to their final stop.

As I exited the bathroom, I called into our providnitsa to say hello and to get a coffee sachet and podstakannik and then filled it with the piping hot water from the samovar. I joined my new friends in our cabin, although space was very much at a premium as Ivan and Nikita were climbing up and down our bunk beds.

My gaze was averted to the outside of our window once more, where everything was still and silent. I no longer witnessed the endless plains of Siberia with their luscious and fertile lands. Siberia has passed now and so too has Asia. The broad canvas of the Urals and European Russia have come into sight but the ever present and mysterious Taiga forest still enthrals the traveller as thoughts of Moscow come to my mind.

As the lovely and aromatic taste of the coffee entered my body, I listened as Alexander began to tell me about the lives of his family. Alexander works as an engineer for Russian trains in Siberia's Krasnoyarsk and they are travelling by train from Krasnoyarsk to Moscow as they received a travel discount as employees of Russian rail. When Alexander's family reaches Yaroslavsky Station in Moscow, they will then travel by plane to Turkey to enjoy their summer holidays for two weeks before returning to Moscow and riding once more along the Trans-Siberian Railway east and home to Krasnoyarsk. I am so impressed with the manners shown by Alexander's children as they treat me with such respect as both a person who is older than them and as a person from another country.

Ivan continued to talk with me about topics that I could not understand and yet we seemed to have a deep connection due to the shared space that we found ourselves to be in. The younger brother Nikita loves all things dinosaurs as he showed me his green coloured toy T-Rex. I didn't have a vast knowledge on dinosaurs but once I said Jurassic Park Nikita's eyes enlarged and an excited youthful exuberance was released within him as he took out his notebook and showed me some of his dinosaur drawings.

As I observed both Ivan and Nikita within our close environs, I began to ponder on childhood and how we mostly look back on it with good or bad memories but rarely do we notice childhood as we actually live through those moments. As children all our senses are heightened as we experience a creative surge within our imaginations as our world and our place within that world becomes apparent to our young minds. When we are children, we are naturally childlike as we view the world from the curious and wonderous eyes of innocence. If we are lucky enough we are raised by caring and moral guardians who open up the world to us with the passage of time. Our young minds are not focussed on the future or about the harsh realities of suffering within our lives. An innocent child takes its very first steps into its own development and such development and learning will stay with these young minds as they exit childhood and into the other world of adulthood. Ivan and Nikita will probably never recall the day they spent with a traveller on the train to Moscow as their young minds are living life to its fullest during these moments. My mind is on other things. It is on the enlightened experience that I gain from such a journey across Russia but if I was a ten year old boy my mind would want to play, to be happy, to laugh, to shout and to run around from cabin to cabin because that is what children do when they are young.

As much as I delight and feel puerile in the presence of children, I know that this person is most happy when he is alone and so I made my way to the restaurant carriage for my final meal along the Trans-Siberian Railway. I was its only visitor and I took a seat beside the window in the direction of the train and Moscow.

These are the moments I love the most when travelling. The moments that I am alone listening to the thoughts within as I move slowly yet steadily to my next destination. There are certain things we do each day and these become part of our behavioural traits. Some people like to watch their favourite TV programme while others will not go to sleep until they read from a book. My day can never be complete unless I write.

Writing is my great solace, my therapy on which to unite the external discord of complexity with the internal wonder. I don't have a computer on which to type words. All I need is my blank journal with my pencil case full of pens. These are the sacred tools for a writer and no writer will ever be without their instruments of creativity. I never fully understood at school why we had to write on lines within our copy books. Lines on a page stifle creativity. How come our teachers never knew that? They talked about how neat our writing should be within the columns but no true writer will ever accept such nonsense. The blank page in front of a writer is the building blocks of all writing. When I turn on a computer and write a piece on Microsoft word, I do not see any lines. If I receive a typed letter, there are no lines under the sender's words. Pasternak's *Dr Zhivago,* which rests on the table beside me, does not have any lines.

Writing words on a blank page for a writer shares the very same ideal with a painter on which their canvas rests before the moment of creativity begins. For a writer, it all begins when the blank page is revealed and it faces the writer. In those moments, all writers have a choice. They can ignore the blank page, get up and walk away or they can face the blank page and smile within as they realise how lucky they are to be alive at such moments in life. There is nothing to fear from the blank page. Procrastination is often used to explain away a writer facing the blank page but there is no logic in such an explanation. The blank page is to be celebrated for a writer for the very fact that the writer has even got to this moment sitting down with a pen in his hand. The blank page for any writer is base camp with eyes fixed up at the wonderous and inconceivable Mount Everest. It begins with just one word, any word and so the journey follows a writer from a blank page as he slowly turns inwards to meet with the internal creativity on which to surge to the external canvas. The writer needs space, solitude, patience and a true desire to create. As the moments move onward words on a page begin to fill and there is no blankness behind a writer. The blank page will always exist ahead of the writer but the writer must believe that the words will come because he calls them from within his own silence.

Time slipped away so suddenly as I nourished my body with a plate of potatoes and mushrooms and I nourished my soul with new words onto a page as the train continued on its own journey westward. I returned to a quiet cabin with only Christina sitting on Alexander's bed as she was making up Makar's warm bottle of milk for the coming evening.

'I want to practise my English with you,' said an excited Christina as I sat down on my bed.

'You speak good English,' an impressed native English speaker said in reply.

'My mother is an English teacher back home in Krasnoyarsk,' said Christina. 'She was born in Ukraine as was Alexander's grandmother,' echoed Christina.

'Slava Ukraine,' I proudly said in reply.

'Slava,' a puzzled Christina said in reply. 'Do you know Ukraine?' asked Christina.

'Yes, I do. I first visited Ukraine back in the summer of 2014 and I got to experience Kiev, Chernobyl, Odessa and Uman,' I proudly stated.

'Chernobyl?' a horrified Christina shrieked.

'Yes, yes, Chernobyl,' a smiling traveller responded.

'Are you crazy?' a worried Christina asked.

'Probably,' I responded. 'I could not visit Ukraine and avoid its most notorious place,' I stated.

'26 April 1986,' a nostalgic Christina responded.

'Yes, all the world knows that date now,' I said.

'It was the Soviet Union then,' said Christina.

'I stood a mere 200 metres from the doomed reactor 4 at Chernobyl,' I said.

'I could never visit there,' said Christina.

'I walked through the ruins of Pripyat city,' I sadly responded.

'It was a city for 50,000 people and it was built in 1970 only to fall in 1986,' said a despondent Christina.

'Everything that is there is left as it was on that fateful day in 1986,' I said.

'What part of Ukraine did you go to on your second visit?' asked Christina.

'I spent seven nights in the old town of Lviv arriving on New Year's Day earlier this year,' I said.

'Oh lovely, lovely Lviv,' responded Christina. 'I will go there one day with Alexander and my children,' a determined Christina stated.

'I really loved Lviv, Christina. There is something so charming, so cosy and so calming about old towns in Europe,' I said.

'Was it snowing when you were in Lviv?' asked Christina.

'Yes,' I excitedly responded. 'There were blankets of snow so thick that my feet had to crunch through its hardened surface to manoeuvre around Lviv,' I said.

'Haha. If you want to experience snow, then come to Siberia in January,' said Christina.

'What part of Ukraine was your mother born in?' I asked.

'Kharkiv in eastern Ukraine,' responded Christina.

'I never made it eastward,' I said.

'If you want to know a country and their people, you need to experience all of its regions,' said Christina.

'What part of Ukraine was Alexander's grandmother born in?' I asked.

'Kharkiv too,' said Christina. 'You see, Ukraine is in our soul. The blood running through our veins is both Russian and Ukrainian. We are Slavic people,' a passionate Christina said.

'Have you ever been to Belarus?' I inquisitively asked.

'No but White Russia are our Slavic brothers and sisters,' said Christina.

'Yes,' I responded as my mind drifted outward.

'Have you ever been to Belarus?' a curious Christina asked.

'Yes, many times,' I responded. 'I knew a girl from there once,' I sadly responded.

'Did you love her?' asked Christina.

'Yes I did. I loved her very much but our loved died a long time ago,' I painfully remembered.

'I am sorry,' an empathetic Christina said softly.

'That is OK,' I said. 'The pain within my soul is comparable with the great love we shared for such fleeting moments,' I said as my eyes and heart looked outward as the train hurtled along past the numerous log cabins with their patterned and flowing smoke rising upward in the stillness of the summer air.

'Did you have any children together?' asked Christina.

'No,' I said in reply.

'Oh, how sad,' said Christina. 'Family is everything for Slavic people,' confirmed Christina.

'Yes, I know that,' I replied.

'You can love again,' an encouraging Christina said as she looked directly into my soul.

'I don't know about that,' I hesitantly responded. 'There are many kinds of love in this world but only her love elevated my heart and resurrected my soul the most,' I responded as a tear drop fell from my moist eyelids.

Christina was just about to respond when Makar came racing into our cabin on his hands and knees and the moments of nostalgia and longing passed into the quietness of the evening.

Our cabin fell silent as Alexander switched off our light at 20:30. Both Ivan and Nikita had already fallen asleep as the day's activities and the energy spent within carriage 10 had rendered their bodies into a calming stillness. I turned onto my stomach and rested my chin upon the pillow as I looked out at the enduring light as the golden sun was about to set in the distance.

All was quiet and still. The only sounds were the churning of the propellers that continued to move our train to its final stop early tomorrow morning. As the fading light gave way to a darkened night I rolled over onto my back and with eyes brightly opened and my mind alert with my thoughts, I stared up at our ceiling and passed away those final few moments of happiness and freedom riding the great trains across the boundless plains of Russia.

When I am an old man with my physical body declining, I hope to be seated in my rocking chair with arms outstretched to be heated by the open and crackling log fire. I hope the old man with a calming smile across his withering face will remember this moment as his young self was truly free, happy and accepting of his place in this ever changing world of ours. If the old man could reach out to the past and to this moment, he might say to his younger self:

'Go out there and live. Live your best life, be free and always be curious about the world around you. Do not sleep for too long. You can sleep for a thousand years when you are dead but your heart beats now, your mind is at work, your body is young and you are restless. Do not hurt or interfere with your fellow human beings. Be kind and gentle to animals as through them we are given a window into the soul of our creator. Protect our natural world, for it has lived long before we arrived and it will continue to live long after we have departed this world. Roam this earth because it is the only home you have ever known. Come out from your house, your community, your village, your towns and cities, your nations and see the whole world as your home and your family. Travel the world and especially to new places because when we continue to see and experience the world in new ways, we slowly begin to break down the barriers that divide us. Spend time with new cultures and people who are different to you because when we do so, we begin to accept our differences and we slowly eradicate the hate and division that is incessant within our hearts. You must protect your body, which encompasses your mind and soul. You have but one body and it is yours and only yours for the duration of your life. This is the gift of life. You must protect your body, nourish it, open it up to the magic of the world around you with its great wonders and wisdom that you need to learn in order to become the person that you are supposed to become. You must first love the core and spirit of who you are. This is your first test. You then break the ego that lurks within you and you accept yourself as you naturally are. Only when you find the equilibrium within yourself can you then begin to accept and love others along your journey through life. This is when your life becomes really exciting as all your senses are switched on manually by you its keeper and protector. They become heightened and for the first time in your life you begin to see it in a new and everlasting way. That is the moment when your former life of anger, hatred, division, a life of monotony and endless days and nights passing by suddenly and without warning dies and a period of metamorphosis begins until a new resurrected soul of harmony, unity, acceptance and most of all love begins to live a new journey for you and in you. Never see time as your enemy. You must accept time for the role it plays in your life. Time cannot be measured; it cannot be bargained with. Instead, live your life to the fullest with time as your constant companion. And remember this above all else: the time on your clock is ticking and has been doing so ever since you first breathed the air in this world within your mother's womb. It will continue to tick but one day in the future which will eventually be your present, time will stop for you, your body will fail you as it must do in order for you to pay back for the sins of your humanity. When that day comes as it is certain to do you must embrace your impending death and let it pass into the stillness of the earth but in knowing that you truly lived the best life that you could during your gift of life. It all comes down to one thing, one word, one feeling but this feeling changes all the world instantly and permanently. That word is love. You must love even when you are put to the test. You must love even when you are hurt, humiliated, saddened, grief-stricken, lonely, rejected. You must love when you are suffering and at your weakest and know that such moments will pass and the sun will shine again for you. And there you have it my younger self. Love is what you must do in order to solve the puzzle of life. Oh, one more thing my friend. You must write!'

The traveller with his heart and mind open to the magic of the unknown slowly drifted into a deep sleep and began to dream of his next adventure.

Chapter 19
Moscow

As train number 99 crept slowly into Yaroslavsky Station in Moscow, it was time to say farewell to the Trans-Siberian Railway and to the family that have been part of my life ever since I departed Yekaterinburg.

So often in our lives when we achieve something of value, those moments are tinged with sadness and a feeling of anti-climax remains as there is no outward euphoria. There are no guests waiting along the platform cheering my arrival in Russia's capital. There are no special awards for an achievement having crossed the length of Russia by train. Nobody knows me here. I am just another face in the crowd. As I carried my suitcase and backpack off the train one final time I am reminded that the true accomplishments in life should be experienced internally with a silence, a humility and a true sense of happiness by living each moment in time without any expectations.

When I set out from Vladivostok one month ago, I never wanted to imagine my journey's end in Moscow. I wanted to experience each moment as a continuous journey so that I was part of each narrative, part of each experience and that I gave myself fully to the stimulating rather than pondering on what will come in the future. There is a danger in looking too far ahead because it is just today and specifically now that is all we can control and be part of because even tomorrow will be today when we arrive there.

I shared some final moments with the family from Siberia as we captured a few still images for our memories to look back on. I noticed that young Ivan was not very friendly with me on parting but at his tender age we are still developing our minds and our bodies to the events that we experience. I am reminded so often in life that people come into and out of our lives in quick succession and even our memories of such people will fade with the erosion of time.

We just shared a space together for a brief moment during our lives and whilst we brought laughter, friendship and happiness for one another during those brief hours together in the end like so much else in our lives these moments will be consigned to and forgotten in the past.

I am back in Moscow once more. The last time I was here was at the end of the summer of 2011 with John the Ranter after I had completed my thesis and we then made our way south to the grave of Tolstoy at Yasnaya Polyana near Tula. There is a feeling of calmness with familiarity on returning to a place that we once knew.

For the next six nights, I will be staying at the Matreshka Hotel in Teatranya Ploshad in close proximity to the Bolshoi Theatre and Red Square. I am staying in room A221 on the second floor of a building next to the Matreshka Hotel. My room is similar to the room I had in Prague many years ago, in that it has two storeys. On the ground floor exists my bathroom, shower, a wardrobe and a small grey couch on which to rest under the stairs. The winding stairs lead to a wooden banister and behind it are two single beds.

After a short rest in the darkness, it was time to enter the light of Moscow. There is often an anticipation that resides within a traveller before stepping out onto the streets on arrival into a city. My mind has accumulated and experienced thousands of images over the past few weeks along my journey but I am reminded that although the Trans-Siberian Railway journey has completed my own journey and experience continues to evolve with the march of time.

Summer has already arrived in Moscow as I read a temperature gauge of 25C. I made my way down Teatranya Ploshad, passing the ever present, the most elegant and radiant, gleaming under the intense heat of Moscow, its graceful Bolshoi Theatre. I crossed over and peered up at a statue of Marx that I recall from my previous visit to Moscow. This man played a pivotal role in a country that was not his own and yet how his grand ideal of the collective working together to build a nation was in the end distorted and destroyed by the antithesis of communism. Perhaps we cannot live with such ideals that Marx and Engels laid out for us.

Is it in our nature to destroy one another? Communism utterly destroyed the soul of the Russian people because the enemy was no longer Napoleon or Hitler but it was the silent enemy, the whispering of a neighbour passing the gentle breeze into the Kremlin. Silence and darkness were the great powers of the Soviet Union under communism. To have been a free-thinker and dissenter was to have been an enemy of the state and the crushing chains of the gulags awaited such actions. Maybe Yuri was correct when he stated the murders of the Romanov family killed the soul of old Rus and it then fell into a pit of darkness and blood similar to the pit where the remains of the Romanov family were thrown into. We can all prepare for an enemy before attack because we can anticipate their moves but how can we prepare for an attack that is waged within our own homes by our own people?

Communism never actually began. Its ideals were too sacred to be implemented by the corruption of our own souls. If a young boy or girl in the 21st century were to look up at the statue of Marx, they might ask, 'Who is the old man with the beard?' What answer could their confused parents give in response? The revisionist historian will continue to make such negative claims about Marx but the truth rests in his words and in an idealism that was centred around and for the individual. Capitalism revolves around the individual and how that individual can gain a financial wealth but it is always an external wealth that can never answer or calm the questions that lay internally. The capitalist can never fully be satisfied because the external financial rewards will never be enough. If the capitalist earns one million euro, then two million euro will become the next goal and then onto five million and ten million whereas in Marx's ideal the one million euro would be collectively shared so that all the individuals will gain but only as part of a shared collective.

I walked the short distance onto Red Square passing the familiar red bricked History Museum and as I stepped onto the cobbled stones, I looked up and there she was in dazzling effervescent colours as she has stood throughout the turbulent past of Russia's history. She stands erect, proud, powerful and amongst the beating heart of Moscow. She is St Basil's Cathedral. Russia's seat of power, the Kremlin always has her spellbinding image in their sights.

Below the Kremlin at ground level is Lenin's embalmed body in the closely guarded mausoleum next to the History Museum. As I strolled around this sacred square I was struck at how a 20th century icon and communist in Lenin meets 21st century ostentatious capitalism in the Gum Department Store. The never-ending opulence of designer products is continuously open for business with their lights shining in all the mansions whereas the grand idealist of communism lays dead, mummified with his doors closed and lights switched off. Capitalism is truly alive and there is a sense of goading as she stands aloft, looking across at her dead predecessor. How long more must the Russian people wait for

Lenin's body to be removed here from Red Square and buried into the earth which would be a fitting and natural end to a life? There is an internal paranoia about a state who keeps a permanent and physical reminder of their past encased for visitors to come in and pass this once leader of Russia in an air of reverential stillness and then to depart never fully understanding what was the meaning of such a moment. When we depart this earthly world and relinquish our body, we are no longer in control and so it is the decisions of others that will determine either the release of our physical body into the earth's soil or a scattering of our burnt remains into the atmosphere. It is only the very unlucky souls like Lenin and Ho Chi Minh that continue to exist as cold statues for the voyeuristic delights of the masses. I wonder did anyone ever ask Lenin the man where he would like to rest on death?

I admire the life and death of Lev Nikoleavich Tolstoy because although he was excommunicated by the Russian Orthodox Church and consequently refused permission to be buried on consecrated ground, he left instructions for his family to give him a very simple funeral in a small and unmarked grave on the grounds of his home at Yasnaya Polyana. Tolstoy can rest in peace and in silence under the tall fir trees whistling in the wind whereas Lenin continues to live his nightmare under the glass on Red Square.

The traveller set out on foot and in exploration in Moscow's midday heat. I made my way down to Arbat Street passing the Dostoyevsky statue as he was perched outside the state library. Behind Arbat Square lies one of Moscow's oldest streets, which is a two-kilometre pedestrian street called Old Arbat. It is a street that was once frequented by Pushkin, Gogol, Tolstoy and Gorky. Pushkin lived at number fifty-three Arbat Street and Gogol lived nearby at Nikitsky Boulevard. This once enticing and idyllic street with so much history, tradition and character would not be recognisable today to any of these great writers. Arbat Street reminds me of the Champs Elysses in Paris and how that once quaint boulevard is now consumed with fast-food restaurants and tacky tourist traps. Old Arbat today is dominated by tourist souvenir shops and the people who work in such stores are constantly on the lookout for passing custom.

I am not interested in such frivolous places that cannot stimulate my mind. I walked down Old Arbat until I came to Pushkin's former home, located in a quiet corner at the end of Old Arbat. Its green exterior hue guided me inward as I paid the 250 rouble entrance fee to immerse myself into Pushkin's former home. There was a Russian lady in each room of the museum that I entered and they always kept me in their sights to ensure that I did not take any photos in the esteemed home of Russia's father of literature. There are many windows in this former home and briefly as I looked down onto Old Arbat I imagined Pushkin alone at his wooden writing desk and then suddenly rising onto the creaking wooden floors only to peer outward onto 19th century Arbat. I am briefly reminded that the passage of time distorts the image that both Pushkin saw and that I see now of Old Arbat from this very same room.

As I continued to look out onto Old Arbat, I began to imagine the contact that both Pushkin and Gogol had whilst their literary lives collided and fused during the 19th century. Lightning did strike twice with first Pushkin succumbing to death in a duel and his rightful heir, Lermontov, suffered a similar fate and those two momentous events marked the passing of Russia's romantic age. It was followed by the dawn of Gogol, the supernatural, which was then followed by the dark and inward struggle of man envisaged by Dostoyevsky.

I departed Old Arbat and walked across from metro Arbatskaya to find Gogol's former home at number seven Nikitsky Boulevard. Whereas Pushkin's former home is green in colour, Gogol's is a bright yellow. On entry to the museum, I received a handbook in English detailing the various rooms that I would enter. A writer likes to immerse oneself into the private and creative domain of another writer. A writer likes to walk on the very same floor as another writer to feel the inspiration and to be enraptured in order to continue the creative surge that they left behind on departing such a room. Gogol wrote his manuscripts here at number seven, although he also burnt his manuscript for his *Dead Souls* also in this home and relinquished his once life to death also at this very space in Moscow. On the walls are memories captured in the time of Gogol and with his literary friends, including Ivan Turgenev, who also frequented Gogol's home during his lifetime. I spent time in Gogol's former bedroom, which had a shutter next to his bed. A person's bedroom is an inviolable space where the person is most vulnerable in this world. It is a place of unprofane sanctity from which to retreat from the outside world in between the creative moments spent at the writing desk. I saw Gogol's death mask and also his overcoat, which are reciprocal with his life and writing but remain on as physical reminders from a life once lived. I read Gogol's final words written in this life as he mentioned something about taking the stairs again. Who knows what goes through the mind of a person during their final moments before death arrives and brings the life of the person away in the silence and within the mystery of such transitory moments?

We are very much present at the beginning and at the end of our lives but we cannot control either moment. We become a witness of the light as we enter the world and to the darkness on departing our corruptive state in the hope that maybe the light will return once more. I ordered an apple juice from the Gogol café next to the museum and ventured outward to the courtyard to quench my thirst whilst looking up onto the Gogol monument that Stalin did not like, as it depicted Gogol in a decrepit physical manner. I like this monument of Gogol precisely for the reason that Gogol is depicted as physically frail because frailty is a feature common to all writers but not necessarily in a physical manner. I departed Gogol's former home and made my way up along the tree-lined avenue to Pushkin Square. I sat on a wooden bench on this sweltering summer afternoon and peered upwards at the monument dedicated to Pushkin. I imagined the historical and literary significance of the unveiling of this monument to Russia's slain poet. Dostoyevsky once stood here in reverence with his body and with his words to honour a hero of old Rus. Pushkin is no longer here nor are Dostoyevsky and Gogol either but a part of a person remains on and alive amid the places that once was traced by their footsteps. The physical person is no longer here and can never be here again but the ideals that these men as writers stood for will live on through the consciousness of the people who choose to inherit such ideals.

Following a day walking the streets of literary Moscow, I retreated to an Uzbek restaurant on Ulitsa Neglimaya. It is a restaurant that I know well as John the Ranter and I frequented its doors during our last visit to Moscow. I sat at a table outside on the veranda overlooking a main road on this balmy evening. The abiding memory that I hold from when John the Ranter and I spent time at this restaurant is how customers while enjoying their meal were treated to the hypnotic rhythm of belly dancers as they glided so effortlessly to the exotic sounds of this ancient dance form. During our final meal at the Uzbek restaurant, the manager came to our table and asked if we had enjoyed our meal. In a tone of sarcastic sadness, John the Ranter replied, 'The food was delicious as it has been throughout the last week but we feel sad as we never got to see the belly dancers.' At that very moment, the manager on observing our facial expressions clicked his fingers and suddenly two satisfying ladies clad in glittering silk, long flowing hair with bronzed torso's revealing slim lined curved bellies and white high-heeled sandals which elongated their taut bodies arrived to the sudden hypnotic sounds from the east. I looked over at John the Ranter as our eyes met and a burst of laughter fell outward from our happy faces. On exiting the restaurant on that night, John the Ranter proudly proclaimed our satisfaction to the manager in saying, 'We are happy now that we got to experience the belly dancers' to an equally happy and satisfied restaurant manager.

I sat down to enjoy a freshly cooked meal of vegetable borsch soup with a vegetarian dish of rice and roasted vegetables alongside freshly squeezed apple juice. It was my first home cooked meal since I departed Yekaterinburg and both my mind and body turned to the sumptuous delights that covered my table and I rejected the visual delights of the belly dancers as they danced inside the restaurant to the excitement of the other customers.

I set out on foot in the direction of southwest Moscow as the blistering sun shone downwards amid the cloudy skies. My first stop was to Christ the Saviour Cathedral on the hill overlooking the Moskva River. This house of sanctuary and worship with its welcoming golden cupolas emanating outwards as it welcomes all into its ornate icons spread across its walls enticing a visitor to stop, ponder, pray and be mystified while its soul gives way to the piercing scent of burning candles.

As I observed the many people enter and exit such a building, I am reminded that such places of worship were forbidden during communism when God was replaced by the Soviet state as its head and saviour. The Russian soul has never forgotten Vladimir who brought Christianity to old Rus just like how St Patrick brought Christianity to once pagan Ireland. Both Russia and Ireland owe a lot to the Christian pioneers of Vladimir and St Patrick. Their message was the very same message that Jesus preached during his years of ministry before the final assault by the darkness and evil of mankind. As I stood inside the marble floors of the cathedral my eyes were drawn upward to its many and polished murals and frescoes. I have seen the interior and exterior of many Russian Orthodox Churches and cathedrals on my travels across Russia and it dawned on me that communism continued to preach a collective working together of man but the lie was sold to an unsuspecting people. The great irony is that it is such places of worship like Christ the Saviour Cathedral that draws people in as a collective because of a simple message of love for one another. That was the original message of communism as conjured up by Marx and Engels before it became contaminated and stained by the actions of man.

Upon departing Christ the Saviour Cathedral I wandered along the Moskva River southward to Gorky Park as the Scorpions Wind of Change resonated with my thoughts and memories. The song and its words followed along my journey as I walked in the sweltering midday sun. I remember watching the video of that song as a young boy and seeing the streets of Berlin and Moscow. I did not understand the politics between Germany and the Soviet Union but I was taken inward by the visceral images of history and the moving rhythm of the lyrics that both captured my imagination and allowed such an imagination to soar and be free. Today, I am a free man roaming the streets of Moscow. There is no longer a wind of change hovering over this city and its people or at least it is not visible to my eyes. Russia no longer lives with shackled chains but are any of us truly free in this world? Maybe freedom is all an illusion and the chains that we carry are the invisible ones that weigh down our bodies and our souls. I came upon Muzeon Park with their large collection of statues and memorials that were once standing proud and tall during the Soviet Union. When communism ended, so did such memories of its past and now they are part of an outdoor museum as a form of nostalgia for an age that promised so much but delivered a permanent scar to the soul of the Russian people. I stood alongside statues of Pushkin and Lermontov, both in close proximity to each other, just like the parallels in their lives and in their words. I am a little unsure as to why the poets of Russia's romantic age stand here next to Soviet statues but perhaps the Russian state wanted to incorporate something of substance and of historical importance rather that portraying the mundane Soviet monuments that are scattered throughout this park.

I crossed the road and made my way into Gorky Park. I paused for a moment to admire the grandeur and elegance of this truly Muscovite park named in honour of a man who straddled between the ages of aristocracy and communism but who always aimed to find a permanent truth through his ongoing search for knowledge. I take delight in Russian parks as there are always so many benches available to sit on, just like they are on display in Parisian parks. Muscovites and Parisians share a common interest to retreat from their everyday existence into a world of their parks where just for a few moments they can be amongst nature and be free to live in the moment of life. I sat for a while beside a small pond and fountain and watched a mother dry her daughter's drenched hair and body after the young girl was swimming in the pond. The love that a mother has for her children cannot be measured in this world. Her love is too pure and beyond the realm of inquiry. This mother carried her child within her womb, protected her until the time came for her to deliver this delicate baby into the world. She then nurtured her so that the child knew instinctively who her mother is. This mother will never stop loving her daughter because she created this life from the depths of her own body and would easily sacrifice her own life for that of her child.

A mere few feet away from the mother and child sharing a loving moment I saw two young boys with Kalashnikov toy machine guns in their hands as though they were in a battle together. Is there any hope for our humanity when our children continue to be slaves to this grand design of division within humanity? Mikhail Kalashnikov is held in such reverence, esteem and pride in Russia but what about his creation, a machine gun that when placed in the hands of humankind destroys the meaning of that kinds humanity?

There is no value to our world and its dream for peace when such weapons of sheer terror exist. When I was a young boy about the same age as these two Russian boys, I too played with toy guns and was lured in by the sheer display of idolatry for these weapons through the many movies that depicted a continuous battle between ourselves. Has anybody ever asked or carried out scientific research to show exactly the impact the bullets of a Kalashnikov machine gun make as they enter the impotent bodies of our species?

These bullets that are manufactured throughout the world when fired from a gun rip through our human flesh and cause catastrophic destruction to our internal organs whose only aim it is to protect our bodies. These organs are no match to the agents of death. The two boys are unaware of the magnitude that exists within such weapons and only see the pleasure of playing together as their true happiness but how many boys who once played with Kalashnikov toy machine guns grew up to handle a real weapon of destruction? When we place such a weapon even as a toy into the hands of our young and developing children, we directly send them a message that such weapons are acceptable in this world because we created them. Throughout the 20th century, the AK47 was continuously pitted against the M16 in order to find out which of the two were the best weapon. We didn't find out which was the better weapon because that is unanswerable due to its internal ludicrousness but the battlefields of the 20th century are covered with the blood of our people fired at by such destroyers of life. How many mothers and fathers had to bury their sons who returned home in body bags and later draped in their national flag all because their lifeless bodies were destroyed by such agents of evil?

When we place such a weapon into our hands when it is fully loaded, then sooner or later somebody will die at the hands of the machine fired at by the coldness of the human machine. Nothing has really changed from the 20th century to the 21st century as humans still use these weapons in their millions throughout the world to destroy one another. If we are ever to change and evolve, then we must put down such weapons that divide us and somehow find the solutions necessary in peace in order to unite. The loving embrace of a mother for her child should move us all the more than the subtle division within ourselves.

The sun shone down upon my pessimism as I exited Gorky Park and crossed a bridge overlooking the Moskva. I proceeded due west in search of Novodevichy Cemetery. I have always loved visiting cemeteries. Perhaps the cemetery allows the once lived humanity to enter again when faced with our grief at the passing of our loved ones. I went to the old part of the cemetery in a quiet sub section beneath the diverse foliage of their numerous trees that stand over the graves of Russia's dead souls.

I took some quiet moments of reflection at the final resting place of Russia's literary past—Anton Chekhov, Nikolai Gogol and Mikhail Bulgakov. All three graves are laid out simply and their elegance in death matches the elegance that these writers brought to readers with their creations. Gogol's is the only grave of the three that displays a wooden Orthodox cross. As I stood around the final resting place of these once lived men, I am again reminded of the impermeable nature of all our lives. These three men of literature once had life rushing through their bodies where they were free to look up at the endless skies at the top of the world but now they exist only as lifeless bones in a box beneath the soil of the earth.

As I was exiting the cemetery, I came upon the final resting place of Russia's first democratically elected leader, Boris Yeltsin. Yeltsin's grave is very elaborate with a hand shell casing of the Russian flag on the ground near the entrance. After a century of revolution and bloody warfare, the last days of the 20th century in Russia embraced a new century and millennium with a promise to their people to lay down their weapons and to envisage a new and more open society just like Mikhail Gorbachev had achieved by helping to end the Cold War and Europe's division of the knocking to the ground of Berlin's Wall.

I made my way on foot to metro station Sportnaya and before I went underground, I looked over to the Luzneki Stadium—Moscow's home to C.S.K.A. and a year ago it staged the final of the Football World Cup where France once again became champions of the world by defeating Croatia.

One of the sheer delights for a traveller in a large city are those endearing and voyeuristic moments spent underground casually observing people as they go about their everyday lives. I took the red line back to the beginning station Salarievo and got off the train to perch myself on a bench beside the busy platform. I was not in any hurry; I had no place to be. My plan was to ride the length of the red line all the way to the final station at Bulvar Rokossovoskogo for no other reason than to embrace the journey, even for a few short moments.

Riding the underground across a city like Moscow is very different than riding overground along the Trans-Siberian Railway. Life is frenetic, quiet, distilled and momentary. Everybody is an unrevealed entity and life is lived within each of our own minds, with a multitude of images continuously passing our senses as we move along to our destination.

I got on the train and found an empty seat in the direction of the train. It wasn't long before the train began to pack and overload and still we all remained hidden from each other. I observed a young man across from me beside the door with a delightfully passive and the golden coat of a retriever dog. I looked a second time and I noticed the man was holding a harness lead around the dog's body. The dog was seated touching his master's feet while observing his world by the scents passing his nostrils. As humans, we see the world through our eyes but to man's best friend, they see their world through their sense of smell. This is not just a pet but a working dog who must navigate this train in order to bring his master safely to his destination. The young man with darkened sunglasses was still and faced forward as he waited.

We live our everyday lives as a mystery to one another. We are always there but still aloof and life is lived beneath the shadows of our internal thoughts. The passengers are faced downward into the other world of their phones. They are physically on this train but it is all a blur as the erosion of time slowly moves forward. Life on underground trains brings momentary excitement and entertainment by the melodic sounds of an accordion player as he moved in and out of the train to earn his living. At one of the stops, a tall man entered the carriage. He had blue jeans, sunglasses fitted to his head with a grey sports jacket and he began to speak. Nobody moved in the direction of his sounds and yet he continued to speak. I looked up at him as he casually observed my presence and continued to look throughout the train. He then took off the black cap from his head and went around the train, hoping for some donations. As the train came to its next destination the man exited as quietly as he had entered. The young man and his dog had left unnoticeably too. Their moments on the train were brief but functional. I looked across and observed a young lady with a boy next to her. She had her phone out but was concentrating on the activity of the young boy as he was engrossed with a Spiderman action figure in one hand and a Superman action figure in the other. The playful delights of this boy reminded me of my own childhood when the only question that needed to be answered was: who would win in a fight between Superman or Spiderman? The adults observing such a world of super heroes would of course answer Superman as he has superpowers but in the creative imaginative world of a child this question could provide an abundance of answers each validating a reason why both would win the fight. The young lady called him Misha. I wondered to myself is she Misha's mother and I began to ponder on the life they lead here in Moscow.

The red-coloured line one ended at Bulvar Rokossovskogo Station and this traveller exited from the train too alongside the other nameless passengers. I walked along the platform and came to a stationery kiosk and ordered a coffee and almond croissant to take with me and to sit along the many seats next to the platform. As I sipped on my warm coffee and indulged my croissant I again waited as all passengers must do before their next train arrives. I spoke no words to anybody but observed everybody. This is a microcosm of our daily lives as we fit in our appointments and activities in the presence of the strangers all around us. My final train journey was a few short stops to Lubyanka Station and as I exited the train and made my way overground, I began to think about the young mother and her son Misha from the underground. We came into one another's lives for the briefest of moments yet we never made any contact. On that train journey and along much of my journey across Russia, I witnessed how important and special the mother is to the identity of all Russians. Russia places the mother as the nurturer and developer of her children. The mother is the vital link between educator in the family and the link to the father who carries this link as leader of his family.

Both Germany and Russia have had their own histories intertwined. Their cultures collided through nationalism and eventually a battle that ended with the deaths of their people. One nation refers to itself as the Fatherland and the other nation proudly refers to itself as the Motherland. Perhaps if all nations could live by the nurturing love of its mother and the guiding presence of their father then somewhere within that family hides the true meaning of what we all seek in this world, a lasting peace.

Chapter 20
A Waltz

As the sun rose on another day in Moscow, the traveller is aware that his time in Russia is drawing to a close and yet it is these last moments that are the most revered because they are tinged with sadness with the advancement of time. The final day in any place during a journey provides moments of introspection by looking back upon the time and the moments as they were lived.

There is part of me that does not want this journey and continued experience to end, because such moments of undisturbed soothing must now fade into the past and simply become memories for me to call upon in the future. We can rage against the flow of time and even face it in conflict, but none of these will bring us contentment. The only solution is to accept the passing of time and to truly live these precious moments within our present, as any other control is futile.

The present moment that we live has to be the most inviting moment of them all because the moment the sun has risen there is such possibilities for experiences within our soul. What was written yesterday has already been finalised but today we look upon a blank canvas on which to live these finite hours that are here with us now but which will be consigned to the past and beyond our control and lived experience as the sun will set on this day. It could be that we just have one day in our lives but that day must be lived over and over again but the key to such a day is that it should contain something new and of value for us to both experience and to gain wisdom from. Once the day is lived, we can let it dissolve into our past but still, after our rest, we should begin living a new day because the new day will be always our greatest day to be alive. I like to imagine my visit to and journey through a particular place to be experienced just once so that my mind and my senses do not become too familiar with a place. This one time experience creates an aura of wonder within our senses so that everything is new but never so new that we become disillusioned and bewildered of such surroundings.

The traveller must continue to be a guest passing through with his bag resting along his shoulders. This was never the traveller's home but the time that he spent here becomes part of his collective experience. When we remain in a place too long, we no longer see it as it is but we judge such a place from the deep insecurities within our lived experience. A new place should never be judged in such a way. A new place should bring mystery as we slowly take away their many layers to find the experience that will become our own and unique one.

As I was walking along a street close to the Kremlin I suddenly looked up as I witnessed a series of government cars and the front of these cars had small Russian flags attached to it at which moment I suspected the president of Russia was in this car. My suspicion was confirmed on observing people on the street stop what they were doing to wave at their leader. One elderly gentleman who was carrying a small trolley immediately stopped and removed the peak cap from his head in respect to the leader of his motherland. In times past, when a Russian or Soviet citizen would come into contact with the mighty River Volga, they would remove their hat to respect the power of this river. The comparison between a respect for the natural world and one's leader, especially here in Russia, is no coincidence as Russian people have always followed their leader often to the detriment of their own safety. Still, I respect this elderly man and the sincere gesture he has given openly to his leader.

I took a journey back in time to the early part of the 19th century as I went in search of a one-story house with mezzanine that stood out and was different to the other more modern buildings and homes that stand in Moscow's 21st century. There she stood, in a quiet residential area surrounded by new Arbat. I stood outside and admired her warm pastel colours of wood built around its many windows looking onto the street.

The preservation of a home from the past gives us a glimpse and insight into the lives of the people who once lived there but are no more. The man who once lived here left an indelible mark on the literary life of Russia. His life was short but he brought with him a message of introspection, individualism and a romantic ideal that was carried on from Pushkin. His name was Mikhail Lermontov and of all Russia's literary figures his story was the most tragic. He shared this home with his grandmother during the few years he spent here in Moscow as a student. The real treasure to this home is upstairs as I walked along the creaking floor and narrow staircase which led me to Lermontov's former bedroom. Beside the window which looks down onto the street rests the young Lermontov's wooden writing desk where the idealistic boy wrote his verses. The images on the walls are of his literary heroes—Pushkin, Byron, Goethe and Schiller. These writers provided the inspiration that the young Lermontov learned from in order to forge out his own path with his own individual voice through his verse. This home was one of creative artistic expression as the young developing boy began to mould his own identity not only through writing but also through painting and music. In this home rests a self-portrait that Lermontov captured of himself. There is a wonder in the gaze emanating out from his eyes. It demands the artist to look into his soul in order to show on canvas a truth that is rarely seen and identified in life.

I continued to experience Moscow as the time flickered away. I came to Sadovaya Ultitsa with the hope of entering Chekhov's memorial house but as I rang the bell at the gate a lady exited and promptly informed me that the house was temporarily closed for renovations. I looked down and saw that she was wearing purple latex gloves and a navy pair of slippers. My imagination was conjuring up scenes of this lady cleaning the desk and books in Chekhov's writing sanctuary.

There is a place that one can spend time in to rest amongst nature and still be surrounded by Moscow and its busy streets on all sides. Every big city needs such an oasis of sedateness amid the everyday noise and distractions from our lives. In Moscow, this place of restfulness is called the Patriarch Ponds. I took a seat on a wooden bench amid the fir trees overlooking the ponds. The trees stand on all sides as the city creeps into view with the many apartment blocks surrounding the pond. All along the pond there were people sitting in the shade of the enveloping trees as the sun's rays fell onto the waters of this enchanting pond. There was a riveting reflection of the branches in the water that added to the calmness that existed at this place. I observed a family close by as they sat on a blanket next to the water's edge. The mother took out from her wooden basket small plastic boxes filled with the food that this family were all focussed upon. The two young girls have pigtails and a colourful flower in their hair. How tender such moments are and yet all so fleeting. The moments spent enjoying a meal with one's family are the most treasured of all and all the more poignant over time.

There was a sign at the entrance to the Patriarch Ponds that read "never talk to strangers." These were the words of Bulgakov from his classic novel *The Master and the Margarita,* where one of the scenes was set right here at the ponds. I heeded the advice of Mr Bulgakov by not conversing with anybody. I closed my eyes and enjoyed the quiet moments in the shade of the strong Moscow sun.

All my senses except for that of sight were in use. I listened to the constant chatter of human voices along with the intermingling of the barking of dogs, of the screaming of children in playful mode, of the flow of hungry ducks as they clamoured to be first to devour the pieces of bread thrown into the pond, of the flight of birds hovering from above to compete with the ducks for the same sustenance, of the rustling of the leaves on the trees as the breeze spread across their branches. I could catch the warm scent of cooked mushrooms as they marinated with the mashed potatoes. It evoked that warm scent of mushrooms I remember coming out from Larisa's kitchen, the scent of freshly cut grass under my feet mixed with the strong scent from the bark of the trees as they were filled with a multitude of insects all vying for their place in the natural world. I touched the wood of the bench that I sat on. Everything and everyone are in their natural places. My sense of sight is in use too even though it is temporarily closed in the physical world I form images within my conscious thoughts that take me far away from here to a place and to a room that is so familiar to me. I wish to go back there to be sitting next to her now but I don't know how to get there anymore. It is a world and a people that have moved on and I have to move on too but alone with only the memories that I carry away from that room.

I continued on with my journey through Moscow's past along the blue line of the underground, exiting at Partizanskaya Station in the northeast of the city. I walked a short distance and there stood another Kremlin, hovering about the Ismailova Market. I wanted to pick some authentic Russian souvenirs from one of its traditional markets.

As I entered the gates at Ismailova, I left behind the modern 21st century and entered a treasure trove from Russia's past. I turned right and came upon two rows of relics, with hundreds of Matryoshka dolls with varied faces greeting me. I bought two Matryoshka dolls of Russian writers. Alexander Pushkin was the face of one and Anton Chekhov the face of the other. Russia's winter season was next, with a large selection of fur coats and hats and square wooden boxes with painted winter scenes that showed a life from long ago. I walked up the steps and came upon a collection of Soviet memorabilia. I had been transported to 1918 as my eyes were drawn to the gold and silver samovars, portraits of Marx, Lenin and Stalin, Soviet era cameras, kerosene lamps, vinyl records with Tchaikovsky and Rachmaninov. It was a real banquet for nostalgic eyes. I reached for another stairs that led to a room of vintage portraits and postcards. I chose a portrait of Turgenev and one of Pushkin too along with some vintage postcards of Tolstoy. On my way back down the stairs, I came across an Underwood manual typewriter dating from the early 20th century. Its eroded and dated look still possesses the voyeur who imagines striking those keys to create words on a page. In the 21st century, we have computers and technology that far exceeds such capabilities of these work horses but I am reminded of the creations that were produced from such machines. It was time for me to return to my modern life in the 21st century, where everything is fast, instant and often out of control. The past is always there right behind us but still we need to move forward and to find the balance that is necessary in order to navigate this changing world.

The couples strolled in two by two. There is an anticipation in the air of what is to come. The two dragons look down upon Apollo and his horses, who in turn leer down upon the fountain with its continued and elegant flow of water. The sixteen white colonnades stand erect, holding up this proud, this energetic and artistic home for all Muscovites and Russians alike. It has witnessed revolutions, suffered during wars and house fires. She has been a beacon of light and of hope for this proud motherland. She is the ever living and much loved Bolshoi Theatre. A night at the ballet, the opera or the theatre is one of Russia's great cultural events. I took my seat on a bench next to the pretty and colourful flower beds overlooking the Bolshoi. I did not secure a much coveted ticket for tonight's performance but to witness such a spectacle is to be part of this artistic beating heart of Moscow.

As I sit here in the 21st century, I imagined the crowds of people over the last few centuries who witnessed the many performances that took place beneath the walls of the Bolshoi. They saw Tchaikovsky's *Swan Lake*, *Sleeping Beauty* and *The Nutcracker*. They saw Mussorgsky's *Boris Godunov* and Glinka's *A Life for the Tsar*. How many times has Pushkin's *Eugene Onegin* been performed on stage or that of Tolstoy's *Anna Karenina* and Chekhov's plays?

The guests of the Bolshoi take such pride in their appearance as they know they are entering a palace of purity. The ladies look beguiling in their long gowns with their hair flowing in the summer breeze. The men are a picture of cleanliness with their dark suits, white shirts and polished shoes. There is an honour in the behaviour of the guests as they know and realise that a night at the Bolshoi is part of the continued historical ensemble of this jewel in Russia's former crown.

As I took out the two Matryoshka dolls that I bought earlier, I thought about the relationship here in Russia of both Moscow and St Petersburg. These two historical, creative and proud cities remind me of two brothers who continue to compete against one another for the affection of its people. Moscow is the older brother and has always been there and experienced so much of the good but also of the suffering. Muscovites are tough, hardworking, with quiet demeanours but with an internal strength that is subtle to the naked eye. St Petersburg is the younger brother. He was in the shadow of his big brother but in his infancy, his life was directed towards aristocracy and a life of the creative and cultured experience. The younger brother went through many name changes as his identity changed from Petrograd to Leningrad and finally to St Petersburg. Moscow became disenchanted with his younger brother in the 19th and early 20th centuries because he felt that there was overwhelming suffering experienced by Russia's serfs at the hands of the Romanov family. When the city in the north became Leningrad his external life changed but the internal identity remained the same and he would always be honoured as the place which Peter created from the swamps along the boundaries of Russia. These two brothers have more in common to unite them than differences to divide them. Moscow has the Bolshoi Theatre; St Petersburg has the Marinsky Theatre. Moscow has the State Tretyakov Gallery; St Petersburg has the State Hermitage Museum. Moscow has the Grand Kremlin Palace; St Petersburg has the Winter Palace. Moscow has St Basil's Cathedral; St Petersburg has St Isaac's Cathedral. Moscow has the Cathedral of Christ the Saviour; St Petersburg has the Church of the Saviour on Spilled Blood. Moscow has Gorky Park; St Petersburg has Peterhof Garden and Park. Moscow has Arbat Street; St Petersburg has Nevsky Prospect. Moscow has C.S.K.A; St Petersburg has Zenit. Moscow has the Moskva River flowing through it; St Petersburg has the Neva River flowing through it. Moscow has Ismailova Market; St Petersburg has Udelnaya Market. Both Moscow and St Petersburg have Novodevichy Cemetery where their dead rest. Moscow has Red Square; St Petersburg has Palace Square. Therein lies the mystery of their differences and idealism. Moscow continues their struggle for the ideal whereas St Petersburg dreams of their past and a period of high artistic endeavour.

There was a moment when these two brothers came together to unite for their motherland. It was the Great Patriotic War with the Nazis invasion of the Soviet Union. It was a nine hundred day long siege of Leningrad resulting in the deaths and starvation of much of its people. The Soviet Union as a collective with Leningrad as its former imperial capital and the symbol of the October Revolution fought back and prevented the tyranny of Nazism from conquering all of Europe and into the east. The two brothers cast aside their historical differences to unite in order to save their dying culture. Their survival and eventual victory brought peace to Europe once more and a unity amongst all Soviet people. Both cities also worked together in the formation of some of their creative people. Both Pushkin and Dostoyevsky were born in Moscow but it was St Petersburg that formed a backdrop for their creative expression. These two writers brought out the very best in the brothers by showing that a willingness to be open and allowing a freedom of expression can result in the flourishing of one's culture and identity. As both brothers move further into the 21st century the rest of their brothers and sisters throughout Russia will look to both Moscow and St Petersburg as symbols of unity where the rest of Russia can continue to be united. This is most evident in the Caucasus with the ongoing Chechen conflict. We learn more of ourselves from the differences that are released outward but which can be allowed to be expressed in order for a culture to exist in the land and in the spirit of old Rus.

I opened up the two wooden Matryoshka dolls of Russian writers. The first Matryoshka doll contained Pushkin on the outside and then Tolstoy, Chekhov, Ostrovsky and finally Dostoyevsky on the very inside. The second doll contained Chekhov on the very outside and inside were Dostoyevsky, Tolstoy, Pushkin and Turgenev. The interesting and mysterious nature of a Matryoshka doll is that once we begin opening the wooden exterior, a whole world is slowly revealed to us. The individual dolls become smaller as we delve deeper inside to find the inner core. It is large on the outside but small at its centre. The Matryoshka doll is a microcosm of Russia in that we must slowly open its exterior in order to reveal the true meaning of this culture. If we place the Matryoshka doll as a single entity on our desk, we just see one doll but when we take the time to open up each of the wooden dolls, it is no longer one entity but many. The Matryoshka dolls are many and varied, just like how the nation of Russia is immense with many cultures. The smallest Matryoshka doll on the very inside is the crucial piece, as this piece lies next to its inner core. This small Matryoshka is the family of Russia. It is surrounded by many. It is proud, creative and yet vulnerable but this small Matryoshka piece is where the soul of Russia rests and where the spirit of old Rus dreams of returning to one day.

As the Bolshoi filled for an evening of entertainment, I made a final journey over to Red Square as these last moments of experience through Russia come to pass. I stepped onto Red Square as I had one final appointment to make. Across from the History Museum and beside the Gum Department Store rests the fairy-tale red bricked with green domes resting under the golden domes of Our Lady of Kazan Orthodox Church. On entering the church, I was met with the icon of our lady of Kazan who is the protector of all Russia. It had a long and troubled past but this little jewel in the shadow of her big brother St Basil still stands and continues to protect her people. I walked up the steps and entered its doors, taking a seat on a wooden bench along the base of the church. This is the only working and functional church on Red Square. People are drawn mystically to the exterior of St Basil's but it is the interior of Our Lady of Kazan that draws people in because it is a place of solitude surrounded by the golden icons of Russia and the continuous stream of reverence by its people for their God and his mother. I walked up and took my place in a queue to show my respect to this sacrosanct icon. I really admire the faith and the reverential showing of submission that Orthodox Christians give towards their icons. Then it was my turn to show my respect. I blessed myself from right to left as all Orthodox Christians do. I bowed my head in submission and kissed the icon. After a long journey crossing the length of Russia, I felt it was the correct thing to do as often in life we are never fully in control of all facets of our humanity. We sometimes need to accept our own limitations in order to live a more balanced and dignified life. As I exited the little church I noticed that a crowd of people had gathered on Red Square watching a musical quartet with instruments. I made my way towards the side of the crowd in the direction of St Basil's. It was quieter there and I found a resting place on the pavement with my tired feet stretched out among the heated cobblestones as the sun was slowly setting over Moscow. When the sun rises tomorrow morning, I will have departed this city and these lands to return home to my city and the lands of my culture. All of this will be a distant memory and the moments from the last month will remain in my long-term memory. Yet, the sun is still above me and I am here on the golden pavement of Red Square living and experiencing this very moment because this moment is the most important as no other moments are guaranteed for us. I observed two young men with backpacks some metres away from me as they were busy capturing their own memories of Red Square and St Basil's Cathedral. I wondered to myself if these two men were about to embark on a journey across Russia along the Trans-Siberian Railway? What experiences will they have and what memories will they make on their own journey? They don't know me nor I them and yet we share the common experience of a traveller and the ability to move from one place to the next as free men simply because we have a desire to do so.

Directly to my right, I noticed a young boy eagerly trying to exit the clutches of his chair as the allure of Red Square's cobbles becomes an obsession for him. His parents, with a continuous observation on their boy, conversed with each other. I wondered what they were talking about? Are they Muscovites? Do they return here to Red Square regularly to sit and enjoy the evening wallowing away the time in the company of each other? I thought to myself about how lucky this boy is to experience this historical place in his home. This boy can come here regularly with his family and will probably do so for many years to come. This could be a meeting place in the future for this boy with somebody he loves. This could be the place he comes when he needs to think and St Basil's will as ever form the backdrop and the inspiration for such introspective thoughts.

What a truly historical place Red Square is. It has witnessed so much by so many over centuries. How many people have walked amid the cobblestones on Red Square and fell upon St Basil's in awe, staring up at the Kremlin in confusion and apathy? How many came here as children, then returned as adults and then finally one last moment before they departed this world?

Red Square has experienced the full inertia, the full cycle and the many stages of man. They came here to welcome in their leaders. They returned to witness the many military parades in honour of their dead from the battlefields of Europe and beyond. They stood on these pavements to recall a past year and the hope within their soul for a bright new year to come.

Red Square witnessed a continuous change with the seasons. The extremities of heat and cold. The hope when spring arrived and the regeneration of its own during autumn. What would St Basil's Cathedral reveal to us if she were a human entity? She witnessed Moscow at its best and at its deplorable worst. St Basil's remains in good company with the History Museum, with Lenin and its newest resident, the Gum Department Store. I remind myself that I too am only passing through as well. I wonder if I will ever return to this square one day and if I do what will I experience then? How many people came onto Red Square to capture an image of St Basil's Cathedral through art? It is, of course, never changing. It continues to exist and to remain in the exact same spot as it did when the very first stone was laid on this spot centuries ago. We continue to hope and believe that the sun will and must rise tomorrow morning. The alternative for us is degradation amid darkness. Our inner voice and the nature of our lives quietly but continuously inform us that all of this will fade and die one day. These gratifying works of architecture by man have inspired us but still they too must fall, crumble and return to nothingness because that is man's fate.

As I stared up onto St Basil's, I began to reflect on my journey from east to west across Russia. It has all passed now but although my body is tired with the erosion of energy and time my mind has increased with knowledge and the many experiences that I went through have revitalised, encouraged and inspired my soul to continue my journey through life until I can no more. I love everything about Russia. Its size, its history, its suffering, but most of all its people in whom the true meaning and soul of Russia rests. I have always felt a deep connection with Russia. It is inexplicable through words. It is a feeling that is always there and it brings a sense of warmth and equanimity to my soul. Perhaps if there is such a concept as reincarnation, then maybe I was Russian in a previous life or maybe I will be Russian in the next birth and so this journey through Russia has been in preparation for such a birth. Either way, it doesn't really matter as I have an affinity with Russia in this life. I feel a deep connection with the Russian soul and how it was depicted by writers such as Pushkin, Lermontov, Gogol, Turgenev, Tolstoy, Dostoyevsky, Chekhov, Solzhenitsyn, Bulgakov and Pasternak. They showed us the readers through their words what it means to suffer whilst holding onto a small and decisive part of our humanity. There is a truth in their words and they were willing to die in order for such truth to be revealed so that man will finally look at its own reflection in the mirror and be horrified to realise the depths of one's own soul and what resides there.

Once we seek truth in all its forms, we change forever from the person who came into this world. When we begin to live our lives by a truth, then the road map for our humanity is revealed to us. In order to accept such truth, we must go through many changes, both physical and psychological and through both processes, we meet with the spiritual, which is the last of the processes we must pass through before truth is revealed. The belief system of truth challenges us to master the vulnerability within our corrupted humanity. Truth demands much from us. It asks very deep and probing questions and we must face ourselves in order to finally answer such questions. Truth inevitably shows us that we are fated to lose the final battle because death will find us and our life will be no more. Truth also reveals to us that there is a harmony, a meaning with the finite moments of our lives. The acceptance of us to live by a system and a truth value means that we can finally live a life that is worthy of the person with whom we are and a validation of the people who created us to be part of this world. Truth also demands from us that we must live a moral life by the way we interact and treat our fellow human beings and the animal and natural world. A life system of truth is a whole new way of experiencing our world but truth can only be lived from within one's own self. It must be accepted internally in order to be lived externally.

I do feel privileged to be sitting here on Red Square after having completed my journey across Russia. The man that set out from Vladivostok one month ago was different from the man that sits here next to St Basil's this evening. I am, of course, physically the same but I have increased with knowledge through my experiences. I am a better person for everything that I experienced through my senses.

There were many moments of loneliness, especially in the solitude at night but such moments when experienced allowed me to increase with wisdom and to accept all the facets to my everyday existence. I met some good people along my journey who have restored some of my faith in humanity. I remember the man from Belarus who shared breakfast with me along my journey in the far east. I forget his face now. The physical and external are irrelevant. All that matters are the special moments that were shared together along the way. I recall Chinggis, the policeman from Buryatia, who loves Liverpool football club. We spent some moments along the streets of Ulan-Ude. They will soon be forgotten but the message of such moments will carry through. I loved spending time with the family from Krasnoyarsk along my final train journey. Life is certainly more meaningful and those moments are precious that we share with others. When we share such a moment with another, we reveal a small part of our life but more importantly we give a part of our humanity onto another. During such moments, we are vulnerable but the defectiveness in our lives is temporarily forgotten because we reach out to another in order to try and accept the conflict within. I especially loved the quiet and inner moments I spent alone, enjoying and getting to know the person that I am. When I am alone, it allows me the space to listen to the voice within and to be at one with my soul and all of its flaws.

Travelling is one of the most enthralling and life-changing experiences that we can enjoy during our finite time in this world. The Trans-Siberian train journey is not just from Moscow to Vladivostok or westward from Vladivostok to Moscow. It is a journey of transformation for the individual. From inside the train, the traveller can see so much and feel so many emotions throughout this long journey. In an age of modern air travel that can transport an individual to any part of the world in less than a day, rail travel and in particular the Trans-Siberian train journey is the last bastion of romance and adventure that the individual can experience on land meandering through some of the most exquisite, diverse and wild landscapes in this world. The traveller on the Trans-Siberian train lives only in the present moment but what we can do in the present moment can change and shape our future. The past has already been written. We must learn to live in the present moment without any fear. We should always move forward with our lives and the Trans-Siberian train is always moving forward to its next destination. The train is in effect the path of life. The traveller enters at the beginning and moves forward from the past into the future but crucially always living in the present moment. The traveller can witness such diversity in nature. There is the great Volga River, the mighty Ural Mountains, the intoxicating Lake Baikal and the enigmatic Taiga Forest and nature at its most raw and living in the wilds of Siberia. By returning to nature, the traveller returns to the inner voice from our soul. This is the voice that guides us and our ability to be moved by the wonder of the natural environment all around us. The Trans-Siberian train journey allows the traveller to feel and express its own emotions. We are emotional beings and we have an instinct to express what it is that we feel within our soul. The Trans-Siberian Railway links cities, towns and villages across an unending country. It brings people together and unites them. The Trans-Siberian train journey allows the traveller to be free whilst on this path of travel. The traveller has a choice to stay on or exit the train. In effect, the traveller must make their own decision and follow their own path. Forget the Orient Express, forget the Shanghai Express and forget laying on some beach getting sunburned with no stimulation. Choose the Trans-Siberian train journey if you wish to feel alive and emotionally moved by a journey that can transform your whole life by the experiences and emotions you have while on this train journey. No other journey may ever compare to the journey on the Trans-Siberian Railway. It is in effect the journey of life.

At that moment, as the sun was drifting away, I looked up and heard Pachelbel's Canon in D major exuding outward from the musical quartet. It was a splendid and sweet mixture of the cello strings fused with the gentle keys of the piano. It was then that I closed my eyes in this external world and opened them into the internal world beyond the realm. I walked in the direction of the sounds and there in the distance she was standing and walking towards me. She had been with me throughout my journey across this infinite land. I was never truly alone because during such moments that I was silent I listened to that sweet voice that rests next to my broken and scarred heart. The experiences that I had I shared them with her because who else could possibly understand the love that this heart has for her? This was the land that we both were to share together and even though she was not there in the physical sense, the love that we once shared meant that she belonged with me throughout all of those days in the light and the gentle nights in the soothing darkness. She was with me on the far side of the world in Vladivostok before the journey began. She was with me on the train journeys as we moved slowly westward when nostalgia filled the air and happiness entered. She was with me along the banks of Lake Baikal at Listyvanka so that the loneliness I felt and the immensity I saw could be shared in equal measure. She was there in Omsk next to the statue of the lovers when I felt broken but still immersed in the love that we once shared together. She was there to see, to hear, to feel all of those experiences crossing a land as immeasurable as the chasm of the loneliness that dwells within my soul. She was there whenever I witnessed the sweet young love of a couple, the glorious sunrise and promise of a venerating sunset. She rested with me in those moments of sheer bliss, witnessing the natural wonder of Siberia each day. She was there, present as a witness at Ganina Yama with me, to try and comprehend the madness of human cruelty that took place on this now sacred land. She was there late at night when I would retreat to my desk and began to create. At such moments, the creative surge in me was most evident and forever pure because of her internal presence close by. When I arrived into Moscow at my journey's end, she was still there as present as she always was. I don't want my eyes to open now because the internal world will fade and I will then return to my every day and ordinary existence. I walked towards the light that exuded outward from her. She stopped, waited and smiled at me. I smiled back and the moment was fused together as a memory from the past when such experiences were continuous. I held out my hand for her and she came towards me. No words were uttered. It was the space between that became the embodiment of this loving moment. The moments that we cherish and long for the most can only be felt with the heart and not described by the tongue. We danced the waltz along the ever trodden Red Square as Pachelbel's Canon reverberated through our living experience. I held her close. I did not want her to depart from my arms. She had returned there and it was in my arms along my heart that I desired her to be. Without time as a construct I could take her with me far away from here on a journey across Russia once more. We could go to the rolling hills in Siberia and rest there in a cottage and live our lives together as one. We would immerse ourselves into the natural environment from where we would eventually return too. We would create life and love because such life came from within our love. We would grow old together and learn to accept and treasure the moments we share and love as one. The dream ended as the sounds of Pachelbel drifted into the ether and as my eyes opened she began to fade away until only a shadow of her long flowing golden hair drifting away in the stillness of this night. A wide smile remained along my face as I accepted the true nature and suffering of our lives but also that I got to see and feel her one more time.

It was at that moment, as she was still alive in my thoughts, that I took out my journal and pen and began to write. I have finally found the meaning of my life. I know it is one of deep sorrow, impending and impenetrable death but also one of immense experience, happiness and love with a truth. I must now write because writing forms the meaning and truth within me. I can finally proclaim these words: I am a writer.

-END-